INDIANS, CARDINALS AND ROSEBUDS

PROFESSIONAL BASEBALL
IN ARDMORE
1947-1961

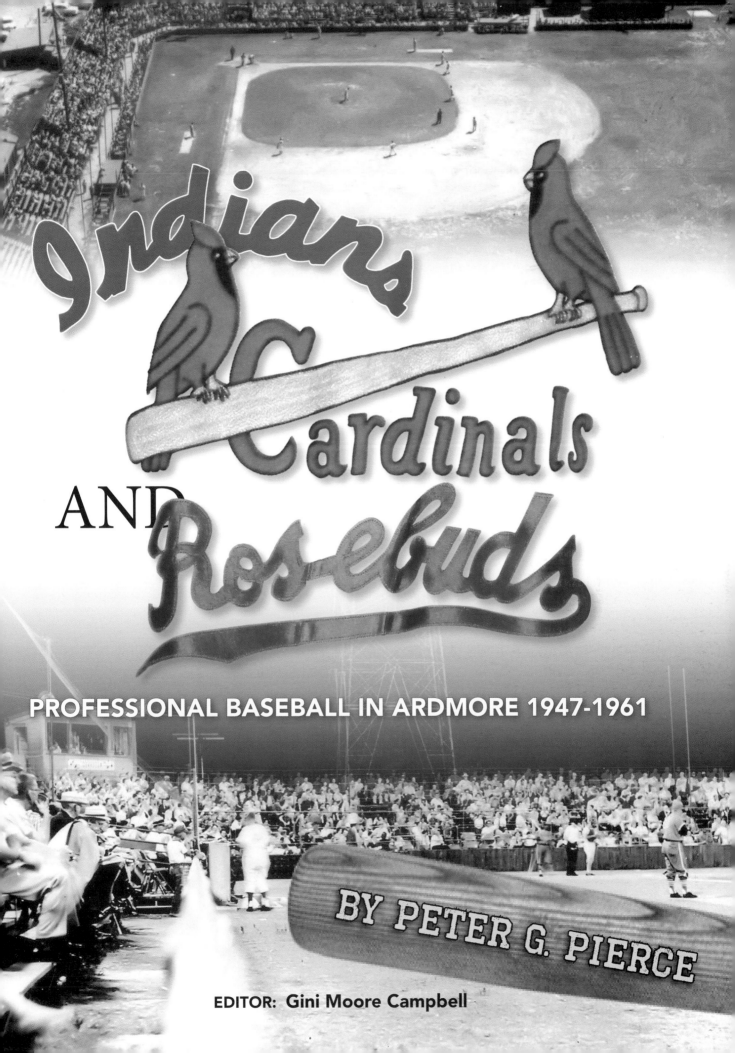

Indians Cardinals AND Rosebuds

PROFESSIONAL BASEBALL IN ARDMORE 1947-1961

BY PETER G. PIERCE

EDITOR: Gini Moore Campbell

OHA

Oklahoma Heritage Association
1400 Classen Drive
Oklahoma City, Oklahoma 73106
405.235.4458
www.oklahomaheritage.com

OKLAHOMA HERITAGE | Association

CONTENTS

PREFACE

Ardmore is where my affair with baseball began with a trip to Cardinal Park to see the 1957 edition of the city's last Sooner State League entry. Finding Carol Daube Sutton's 1949 certificate for four shares of Ardmore Baseball Club, Inc. led ultimately to my first book, *Baseball in the Cross Timbers: The Story of the Sooner State League*, researched and written between 2005 and 2008 and published in 2009 by the Oklahoma Heritage Association. While every city that appeared in that league is covered, the structure is by the people and not the hometowns. There is no one place, for example, to focus completely on, say, Chickasha or Ardmore.

Professional baseball in Ardmore segments nicely into two eras. The first covers the time the Territorians of the Texas League arrived through the day when the Western Association Boomers pulled up stakes for Joplin, Missouri. The second is the period 1947 through 1961 when the Indians and Cardinals toiled in the Sooner State League and the 1961 Rosebuds returned Texas League baseball after a fifty-seven year absence. I have structured the history of professional baseball in Ardmore into two small volumes

This volume, the second, *Indians, Cardinals and Rosebuds*, covers the decade of membership in the Sooner State League and the short 1961 season of the Rosebuds who, like the Territorians, took shelter in Ardmore following flight from their home town. The first, *Territorians to Boomers* tells the story from the time the Territorians took the field as a semi-pro club in 1904 to July, 12, 1926 when the Boomers moved on to greener pastures in the Ozarks.

Indians, Cardinals and Rosebuds contains text adapted from *Baseball in the Cross Timbers* and many of the photos are from it. Subsequent to its publication, however, individuals have given me access to a number of new photos as well as many that became available from *The Daily Ardmoreite*. Additionally, corrections to the text have been made.

While the research and compilations are mine alone, and I am wholly responsible for all errors, both of commission and omission, the people of Ardmore have been instrumental in connection with the writing and publication of this history and *Baseball in the Cross Timbers*. Following a book signing, Barbara Sessions opened a treasure trove of memorabilia and photos from the Waco Turner era and made important identifications. Kim Benedict of *The Daily Ardmoreite* granted permission to expand the photos available to me especially from 1961, the only ones existing from the Rosebuds' sojourn in Ardmore. *Indians, Cardinals and Rosebuds* would not have been possible without the assistance and contributions of Ardmore attorney Derril McGuire who hauled bats from 1951 through 1955. Lynn McIntosh of the Chickasaw Regional Library System again opened her facilities to me and it was there that most of the "grunt" work was done. Gary Farabough, also of the Ardmore Bar, Jeff Gelona and Chris O'Donnell contributed through their comments and encouragement. Finally, Laurie Anne Williams, a descendent of rancher, merchant, and oilman Sam Daube and philanthropist Carol Daube Sutton, has been, as she was with *Baseball in the Cross Timbers*, a great support in this endeavor and her knowledge of the people and history of Ardmore and private archives have worked as a catalyst for ordering the data I assembled.

Peter G. Pierce
Norman, Oklahoma
March 15, 2011

CHAPTER ONE

1947-1952 SEASONS OF THE INDIANS

SEASON	ATTENDANCE	RECORD	FINISH	AFFILIATION	PLAYOFF FIRST ROUND	PLAYOFF FINALS
1947	27,943	72-67	4th	Cleveland	Beat Lawton 3-2	Lost to McAlester 1-4
1948	37,944	60-78	6th	Cleveland		
1949	43,348	57-81	7th	Sherman-Denison (Big State League)		
1950	44,454	75-65	4th		Beat Ada 3-2	Lost to McAlester 2-4
1951	40,742	99-40	1st		Beat Pauls Valley 3-0	Lost to McAlester 2-4
1952	24,362	49-91	8th			

1947

During the more than two decades that followed the demise of the Boomers, Ardmore had to settle for amateur and semi-pro baseball. Strong American Legion teams were fielded and businesses sponsored teams of employees as well as youth ball clubs.

With World War II coming on the heels of the Great Depression, professional baseball all but vanished from Oklahoma. Only Oklahoma City and Tulsa in the Texas League and Ponca City and Muskogee in the

Sam Hale Ford sponsored Little League teams for a number of years. Shown here is a group from the mid-1940s.

Western Association were represented in Organized Baseball. When the Texas League suspended after the 1942 season, the only baseball to be found was in the schools, sandlots, and the several military bases. Base teams included the Enid Army Air Corps Base, whose Enid Airs were finalists in the 1943 and 1944 National Baseball Congress World Series and champions in 1945, Norman Naval Air Station, Tinker Field, Ft. Sill, and Ardmore Army Air Corps Base, the home of the Fliers.

Ardmore's professional team played an exhibition with the Fliers from the Ardmore AFB every year. Shown above is the pre-game ceremony from 1954. Connections with the base were valuable as it was a federal enclave, a place where Oklahoma's prohibition law could not be enforced.

Following the war, Minor League baseball experienced meteoric growth. Millions of fans with money in their pockets, defense workers and veterans alike, filled the ball parks across America. The number of leagues sprang from twelve in 1945, to forty-four in 1946, fifty-two in 1947, to an apex of fifty-nine in 1949. That year 41,872,762 watched some 7,900 players on 448 teams compete for one of the four hundred places on Major League rosters.

Turner came away with the sixth charter franchise which he turned over to a community trust, the Ardmore Athletic Association. Its sole purpose was to provide for perpetuation of baseball in Ardmore. The trustees were William Steele, who led the local Jaycees and served as president, V.E. "Hoot" Gibson, treasurer, Frank Richie, Earl Milam, Ernest L. Massad, Judge John C. Caldwell, and McMillan Lambert. At a November, 1946, League

The 1946 Paris Red Peppers was a founding member of the Class C East Texas League that became the Class B Big State League the next season. The script on the bus is no coincidence. The franchise was owned by the Dr. Pepper bottler in Paris.

Talk of a rookie league in southern Oklahoma had begun before the outbreak of the War. It resumed in 1946 under the impetus of Ucal Clanton and Dr. A. R. Sugg of Ada and Paul Crowl of McAlester. Ardmore was invited to send a representative to an organizational meeting of a Class D league to be known as the Sooner State League. Oil man and Ardmore booster Waco Turner, who had won and lost fortunes, attended the September 4, 1946, affair at the Aldridge Hotel in McAlester. As the dust settled, a six-team circuit emerged with franchises in Ada, McAlester, Seminole, Okmulgee and Shawnee; Lawton and Duncan soon replaced the latter two.

meeting, Richie, Caldwell, Steele, and Murl A. "Dutch" Prather represented the Ardmore group.

Prather was a veteran of twenty seasons in the Minors when he came to Ardmore. A native of Stratford, Oklahoma, he had risen to the top level, Class AA, in 1937 as the regular first baseman for Sacramento in the Pacific Coast League. Most of his seasons, however, were played in Classes C, B, and A. He began managing in 1941 at Pampa in the West Texas-New Mexico League and was coming off a stint in 1946 as the playing manager of the Tyler Trojans of the newly formed East Texas League. He was hired by the trustees of the Association to

Dutch Prather was manager of the 1946 Tyler Trojans.

BELOW: Tribe Park from the north following the 1953 refurbishing by Waco Turner including field boxes, extension of the grandstand, and new bleachers. The new clubhouses, press box and "dugouts" (enclosed benches at the end of the field boxes) were moved to Cardinal Park for the 1956 season. The left field line ran parallel with Boundary Street on the south.

get the franchise ready to play ball when the 1947 season opened. He first served the club as business manager, securing a working agreement with Cleveland of the American League through the Indians' Class A-1 affiliate in Oklahoma City who supplied old uniforms and a few players for Ardmore's use.

The new franchise needed a place to play. Walker Field, a WPA football stadium on the far west side used by the high school, was the only facility available and the local school board was not receptive to a professional team using it. The Association had to come up with another place to play. Under the supervision of Prather, a grandstand and bleachers to be known as Tribe Park was hurriedly thrown up immediately before the 1947 season. The $10,000 structure was located on the old Phillips show grounds, a place where circus big tops and tent revivals had been held, at the then north end of Washington Street at Boundary. The ground was leased through the end of the 1954 season by Industrial Ardmore, Inc., a private corporation.

Industrial Ardmore, Inc. in turn owned the ball park and leased it to the baseball team. It originally seated approximately 1,200 in an uncovered grandstand. The expense of a roof was cost-prohibitive. Prather wore his third hat as talent scout and manager of the fledgling little Indians. Earlier Ardmore teams had sported names such as Browns, Reds, Blues, Giants, Ardmoreites, Peps, Producers, Snappers, and Boomers. The new team was named the Indians due to the affiliation with Cleveland.

The League required that a fifteen-member team have at least seven rookies with the rest being veterans and limited service players. When spring tryouts and drills were concluded, Prather was the only veteran in uniform The rest were raw rookies or players with one or two seasons under their belts. During the season, pitchers Oscar Kuver and Al Blacha, both picked up from Lawton, Roy Burrell, previously released by Seminole, and Mark Pike, later sold to Seminole, were the only players who had played a season in Organized Baseball. As *The Sporting News* observed in its June 24, 1947, issue, manager Dutch Prather was signing every player who could not make another team. But in the Sooner State League that was the situation with most of the other five clubs. The limited working agreement with Cleveland gave the Ardmore club much autonomy but little help on the field. What players Cleveland did send were sifted through the screen of Jimmy Humphries' Oklahoma City Indians of the Texas League.

The Oklahoma City Indians scouted, signed and developed their own players as well as properties of Major League affiliates.

Eighteen position players and eight pitchers rotated through the Ardmore clubhouse. The line-up stabilized by the end of May. Colonel Stephens caught. Popular Bill Hughes was the regular first sacker, being relieved occasionally by Prather. Morris Card held down second base while Harold "Red" Sollars covered shortstop. Jim Hayman, signed on the bounce from Duncan, played third. Robert Andrlik, Homer Smotherman, and Noel Philly roamed the outfield.

Tribe Park was a mess. High grass in the outfield and infield was such that a ball could be lost or a hard grounder stopped. Center field and right field were uphill from the infield while the left field was tilted down. There was deep sand in the infield making it prone to creating erratic bounces contributing to errors. The lighting was bad. Visiting managers from the third base dugout could hardly see their right fielders. During the 1947 season, because of post-War shortages it was several weeks before a switch for the lights was obtained. Until then, an electrician had to scurry up the light poles to turn the lights on and off before and after each game. Sensitive to criticism by Ada columnist Charley Rhodes, Mike Hill of *The Daily Ardmoreite* wrote on June 15, 1947: "Tribe park was built in a hurry by a group of livewire businessmen when use of other parks was denied and the men did a fine job of getting it ready for the season to open." The criticism was valid though.

The Association financed the team's start up by selling up to three trust certificates per person for $100 each; $60 would go to upkeep of the team and $40 for season admission. Season tickets were $40 for sixty-eight games. Hoot Gibson, Ardmore Athletic Association treasurer, reported that after the first nineteen games of the season 7,819 adults and 654 children had attended. Revenue was approximately $5,000. Expenditures totaled $5,127.25. Those were comprised of salaries $3,700, lights and ball park rental $855, public address system $195, eleven dozen balls $162.25, and bats $225. Players were paid between $75 and $125 per month. The team saved the expense of a bus by traveling in private cars and taxis. That proved to be an object lesson in being penny-wise and pound-foolish.

Ragged as the play was, four Ardmore Indians appeared in the July 9, 1947, All-Star game against first-place Lawton: Prather, Morris Card, Noel Philley, and Kuver. Prather was ripping opposing pitchers at a .428 clip at mid-season. He had even won a couple of games using the rule book. On June 5, trailing by a run Ardmore was awarded a forfeit against Ada because there were eighteen Herefords in uniform. President Mealey later sustained Prather's protest of an 8-4 loss also at the hands of Ada on August 9. Catcher Mike Koepka had been taken out of the game but several innings later appeared as the Hereford's third base coach. Final score: Ardmore nine, Ada zero.

Jack Mealey of Holdenville was a career Minor League catcher who began with the 1922 Joplin Miners of the Western Association and finished his last three seasons as manager and sometime catcher for Muskogee in that same league. In between, he reached San Francisco of the Pacific Coast League and spent eight seasons in the Texas League. He was the president of the Sooner State League through 1951.

1948

Prather departed for the greener pasture of Pauls Valley to assume command of that city's new entry for the 1948 season taking with him the battery of Oscar Kuver and Colonel Stephens. The Ardmore nine struggled through 1948 with a sixth-place team and two managers.

Ardmore's fans, like most others in the League, tipped players for home runs and outstanding performances. With the poor officiating, they backed their players. Noel Philley was fined $30, about one week's pay, as a result of an argument with an umpire. The fans passed the hat and raised $28. While it was against League rules for a team to pay a player's fine, there was nothing in the book about fans picking up the tab. Indians catcher Dick Patterson won the distinction of being the first player to be ejected from a Sooner State League game when he was sent to the showers in the second inning of the season opener against Ada. In beating Seminole 28-2 on June 12, the Indians' twenty-five hits and twenty-eight runs set a then-record for the League. The Indians ran wild against Duncan on June 26, stealing fifteen bases on former teammate Howard Dunn and former McAlester Rocket George Abbott. Robert Andrlik had five of those swipes. Prather could also bend the rules. He talked Duncan's Otto Utt into moving a home series against the Indians to Ardmore so Prather could attend the Oklahoma Jaycees convention being held there.

Attendance for the opening season was 27,943, fourth in the six-team circuit, far above Duncan's 8,220 but considerably below Ada's 43,657. Ardmore Athletic Association lost about $2,000 in its first year of operation.

Don Smith moved on to Pittsburg, Kansas in the K-O-M League after Ardmore.

Don Smith, who spent 1947 at Oklahoma City, was selected to try his hand at assembling and managing a team. The day before the season was to begin, he had spent the morning in Marietta, Oklahoma, picking up a supply of bats and took receipt of a shipment of uniforms from Oklahoma City. After a four-hour workout, he opened the boxes to find that the ragged uniforms sent were in worse condition than the ones his players were wearing. He learned that the former owner of the Marshall, Texas, club had thirty-five sets of flannels.

After running down the Indians' business manager who was in Hugo, Oklahoma, looking at a bus, he received the go ahead to buy them. Smith and Cleveland scout Hugh Alexander then drove the 140 miles to Paris, Texas, secured the uniforms and made it back to Ardmore at 2 p.m. on game day. With Mrs. Smith and a couple of tailors ripping off "Ms" and sewing red on navy "As," manager Smith made it to Tribe Park where he distributed jerseys and trousers then conducted pre-game drills. Sleepless for thirty-six hours, Smith took his place in right field. His two errors contributed to the 8-4 loss to Ada.

Four Indians had returned from the 1947 squad. Smith and Jim Cooke, who would suc-

ceed him on July 14, were the only veterans among the twelve position players and nine pitchers who wore the Indians' "A." Limited service players Bob Hutchinson and Lew Pilkington, who was injured in an exhibition game, were the only others who had appeared in a professional game. They assisted thirteen rookies to a sixth-place finish. This was a middle of the pack team hitting .260 and fielding .936 with weak pitching. Indicative of the pitching was Vern Glaser who was 3-3 in seven appearances. He gave up forty-six runs on fifty-one hits along with thirty-one walks in forty innings. He only hit four batters and uncorked but a single wild pitch.

The lighting system at Tribe Park always had been temperamental. Before one of the frequent

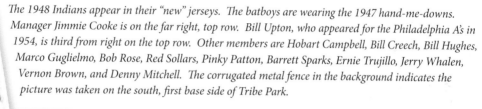

Jim Cooke in 1946.

The 1948 Indians appear in their "new" jerseys. The batboys are wearing the 1947 hand-me-downs. Manager Jimmie Cooke is on the far right, top row. Bill Upton, who appeared for the Philadelphia A's in 1954, is third from right on the top row. Other members are Hobart Campbell, Bill Creech, Bill Hughes, Marco Guglielmo, Bob Rose, Red Sollars, Pinky Patton, Barrett Sparks, Ernie Trujillo, Jerry Whalen, Vernon Brown, and Denny Mitchell. The corrugated metal fence in the background indicates the picture was taken on the south, first base side of Tribe Park.

power failures in 1948, Seminole had runners on second and third. When lights came back on, the bases were loaded. The umpires did not notice until the screaming Ardmore fans pointed to Oilers' manager Hugh Willingham on first base. The umpires chased him to the dugout.

Hugh Willingham managed Seminole from mid-1947 through late 1949. He led the ill-starred 1952 Ardmore Indians as the third manager of the season.

Jess Welch managed his friend Otto Utt's last place Cementers for part of the 1948 season before returning to the classroom. He had been a star for the Halliburton Oil Cementers in the 1930s.

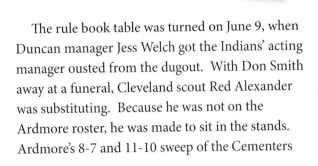

The rule book table was turned on June 9, when Duncan manager Jess Welch got the Indians' acting manager ousted from the dugout. With Don Smith away at a funeral, Cleveland scout Red Alexander was substituting. Because he was not on the Ardmore roster, he was made to sit in the stands. Ardmore's 8-7 and 11-10 sweep of the Cementers

on August 8 turned into a pair of 9-0 losses when Duncan manager Otto Utt protested that shortstop Jerry Whalen and pitcher Ken Johnson were not on the Indians' roster.

Smith at .303 and Cooke with a .285 average were the top hitters while the rest of the position players finished in the low- to mid-.200s. The team managed only twenty-five home runs. Two pitchers had winning records: rookie Ernest Trujillo at 16-11 and carryover Charlie Githens at 5-1. Seventeen-year old Trujillo struck out nineteen Adans and walked only one on April 30, giving up two hits for a 5-3 win. Every Ada batter except two was a strike out victim. First baseman Bill Hughes, who hit .222 in 1947, tried pitching with some success. In his first start on May 2, he batted-in the tying and winning runs to nip McAlester 6-5 on twelve hits. He went 4-2 in 1948. A bright spot in an otherwise bleak season happened on the last day. The Indians ruined rookie pitching phenom, Buddy Yount's, perfect season by handing McAlester a loss in the finale. Despite the poor showing on the field, attendance was up by 10,000 to 37,944. Cleveland dropped Ardmore from its farm system because it had been informed the Indians would not operate in 1949. The arrangement with Cleveland through Oklahoma City was never satisfactory and player aid was negligible.

Players got $2.00-3.00 daily meal money on the road. At home they had to fare for themselves. Bobby Cramer, an outfielder on the 1948 club, took his meals at the Dixie Café. The $5.00 meal ticket literally was punched as used. There is 50¢ left on it.

What the Indians lacked under the ownership of the Athletic Association was a good working agreement, a bus, and a professional business manager. The club spent $4,700 on commercial buses and taxis getting to games. Cleveland stuck them with return train fare for players brought to Ardmore for spring training who were later released. At the end of the 1948 season, Ardmore Athletic Association had a $5,500.04 deficit and no way to pay it. On October, 24, 1948 the trust gave Prather, who had been fired at Pauls Valley and finished the season playing for Chickasha, a ten-day option to buy the franchise, equipment and contracts for $3,500. Industrial Ardmore, Inc., the business entity that had the ground lease and that owned Tribe Park, gave him a forty-day option to buy the facility for $10,724. Prather called a public meeting for October 26; fifty-eight showed up. Prather was unable to close the deal by himself.

1949

Out of that meeting a committee chaired by Ted Alderson was formed to acquire Prather's options. Members were Lloyd Roberts, Albert York, Bob Barnett, J. B. McCullough, Will Abram and Prather. John Judd of the First National Bank & Trust Company of Ardmore chaired a finance committee and bank trust officer Louis Bastin acted as secretary-treasurer. The committee raised $2,125 in cash at the meeting. It was resolved that Ardmore Baseball Club, Inc. be formed to acquire the franchise and lease. The company would offer one thousand shares at $25 each sold through Messrs. Judd and Bastin. Hugh A. Pruitt, a wholesale produce merchant, pledged $2,000. Other wealthy Ardmoreites chipped in $3,000 more. They immediately asked the Ardmore City Commission for a bond election to build a new ball park. The articles of incorporation were filed and on November 29, an organizational meeting was held. Officers and directors were elected by those who had bought shares. Barnett, McCullough, and Roberts were elected to the board of directors as were Eddie Lotz and restaurateur Louis Priddy who would serve as president. Johnny Ferris was hired in March, 1949, as business manager. The board approved

The Ardmore Baseball Club, Inc. only sold 397 of 1,000 shares. This certificate for four shares ($100) belonged to Carol Daube Sutton, a local philanthropist and member of the Oklahoma Hall of Fame.

a working agreement with the Class B Sherman-Denison Twins of the Big State League, which in turn was affiliated with the Washington Senators.

Dutch Prather, unemployed as a manager since leaving Pauls Valley in the cellar, landed the job as the 1949 field general. The change of ownership meant that baseball would be played in 1949 but without a Major League affiliation. With Bill Hughes the only returning player from 1948, Prather was starting from scratch. During his attempt to buy the team, he had negotiated favorably with the Washington Senators whose main scout, Joe Cambria, kept a pipeline of roughly thirty-five Cuban players coming to Sherman-Denison. Lower classification teams were needed to absorb the overflow. Close to Sherman, Ardmore was a natural ally. Nine of the 1949 Indians were products of the Cambria system; their average age was nineteen and one-half. Prather remarked in spring

training "It's bad enough to have to teach these boys baseball. But I've got to teach 'em English, too." Rookie Joe Nodar from Havana, the only one to speak any English, served as translator when the Dutchman could not make himself understood.

Lindbergh Chappoten was a 5'1" right-hander who was signed by Duncan after Ardmore cut him. He remained with that franchise after it moved to Shawnee. When Shawnee had to cut a veteran before the 1952 season, Chappoten was traded to Texarkana for twenty uniforms. Here he is shown with the Duncan Uttmen in 1950.

Lefty Armin Somonte and right-hander Lindy Chappoten were the aces of the pitching staff. Chappoten was 7-2 at Ardmore until released on July 14, while Somonte had thirteen each of wins and losses. Before the season, Prather had boasted that this pitching staff was the best in all Class D; the hurlers proved him wrong. The 1949 Indians were, relative to the rest of the League, an above-average hitting team at .254 and middle of the pack as far as pitching was concerned. They were not the most bobbling collection of fielders Ardmore ever put on a diamond but they were close. They committed 409 errors in 138 games for a .925 fielding percentage but managed two triple plays.

First baseman and pitcher Bill Hughes was a fan favorite. When his daughter was born, the fans took a collection for a layette and hospital expenses.

Language was apparently no barrier between players and local girls. Two of the Cuban players with Ardmore damsels in 1950.

One time their support went too far. When umpire Jerry Pooler called him out at first base, Hughes, as the potential tying run, protested vociferously and got the boot. After the game, which Chickasha won 15-12, Ardmore fans milled around Pooler, threatening him physically. The visiting Chiefs surrounded him and escorted him to their bus. President Mealey fined the Ardmore team $150 for failing to provide adequate police protection and suspended Hughes for three games.

Prather could not make the team gel even after Red Sollars was sent down from Burlington. About all the Dutchman accomplished beyond thirty-eight RBIs was getting the Indians a second chance to win a game that had been lost to Seminole 5-4. Once again, a player who had left the game reappeared in a coaching box. A replay of the last half inning of the game three weeks later did not change the result.

Even though Dutch Prather was back in the Indians' dugout, he could work no magic. The only bright spot was rookie Armin Somonte's 6-0 seven-inning no-hitter against Pauls Valley on June 13. With the team in seventh place the Dutchman was fired on July 25 after the Indians had lost fourteen of their last seventeen games. Rookie Tom McVay, a July 15 graduate of Southeastern State College, was named interim manager. After two days, Duncan's former manager Jim Skidgel replaced him. Skidgel had managed Duncan from June 1 until July 12, between Ed Marleau and Hosea Pfeifer. After Duncan owner Otto Utt gave him the pink slip, he played fourteen games in the outfield for Ada. When Prather was fired, Skidgel solicited the Ardmore job and was allowed to switch to his third team of the season. The change didn't help. The Indians crawled across the line in seventh place.

As part of Prather's separation, the club bought his stock and elected three new directors in hope of improving the franchise's financial stability. Pruitt, shoe seller Raymond Hill, and appliance dealer Dewey Wood joined the five incumbents.

As an independent in 1949, the Ardmore team drew 43,348 who witnessed a 57-81 seventh-place finish. The management of Ardmore Baseball Club, Inc. announced in October of 1949 that the franchise would not operate in 1950 because of an operating deficit of over $5,000 comprised mainly of delinquent federal taxes. A drive to procure guarantors and new money to retire the accumulated debt secured pledges of over $8,000. A shareholders' meeting was held on November 17. Pruitt was present and presented a slate of directors to replace the incumbent board. Oilmen Ward Merrick and Leon Daube, Pruitt, Chevrolet dealer Claud Arnold, Hill, dairyman Ray Colvert, Gene Woerz and Floyd Allen of Ringling were nominated and elected by acclamation. That board never met. Apparently Pruitt had not gotten those gentlemen's consent to be nominated. Several of those elected declined to serve. None of the pledges were honored. The franchise had been turned back to the League.

1950

As 1950 began, Ardmore Baseball Club owned equipment and uniforms, a bus, twelve player contracts, and Tribe Park on land leased by Industrial Ardmore, Inc. Industrial Ardmore had a mortgage on all of Ardmore Baseball Club's property to secure payment of the $8,000 owed on the Park. Arnold, not to be confused with 1950 University of Oklahoma quarterback Claude Arnold, was later convicted of defrauding the State of Oklahoma. Speaking for the controlling interest of Ardmore Baseball Club, Arnold announced that the property was for sale and that the assets would be offered to the highest bidder. The corporation had 397 shares outstanding. Proxies from 227 were collected authorizing a sale conditioned on keeping the team in Ardmore.

Arthur Willingham, of Sherman, Texas, who founded the first post-War Sherman-Denison team in 1946, made a no-cash offer to take out the owners by assuming the debt the Indians had accumulated. With nothing else on the table, on January 14, 1950, he became the new owner of the club by assuming $5,379 of team debt in a transaction that eliminated dissenting minority

Pitcher Mitch Chetkovich (left), owner Art Willingham and new manager Bennie Warren during pre-season drills. The Hardy Murphy Coliseum is in the background. Warren and Chetkovich were the only veterans in Ardmore's 1950 spring camp. Among his other tasks, Willingham drove the team bus.

Monty Stratton (in business suit), a friend of new team owner Art Willingham, threw out the first pitch of the 1950 season in Ardmore. Accompanying him to his right is Queen Nancy Dulaney and her attendants. Player escorts left to right are Stan York, Ernie Klein, and Joe Nodar.

shares. Ardmore Baseball Club executed a deed in lieu of foreclosure to Industrial Ardmore that had the effect of extinguishing the liens. Industrial Ardmore then leased Tribe Park to Willingham for $500 per month, he assumed the ground lease for $400, and agreed to pay insurance of $500. The transaction closed February 1, 1950. He named his son, Bob N. Willingham, to become the business manager and set up shop in the office of Willingham Drilling Company, 30 ½ N. Washington. Young Willingham did not last through spring training. Glenn Snyder, veteran of the Tulsa Oilers, Nashville Vols, and a 1946 player for Sherman, was named as playing business manager. He managed to hit .349 in 129 games and set the League record for doubles with fifty-eight.

Willingham, who held his own tryouts in Cuba, called the shots in the office while Bennie Warren, who had settled in Oklahoma City, was signed to manage the 1950 edition of the Indians. Six Indians were back from 1949 including Cubans Ernesto Klein, Joe Nodar and Armin Somonte. In all, six of his players were Cuban. Many of the rest had prior ties to Willingham from his ownership of East Texas League and Big State League teams. Veteran pitcher Mitch Chetkovich, who had a cup of coffee with the Phillies in 1945, was 12-7 on the mound and led the throwers in batting at .323. A novel experiment at the end of the season paid off. A double header on Labor Day was split with

Armin Somonte was a winner on Player Appreciation Night in 1950. Somonte is third from left. Others are L-R Bennie Warren, Justice of the Peace and announcer Puny Sparger, Somonte, Joe Nodar, Jack Wilson, Marv Hochendorff, Ernesto Klein, and Maurice Bridge.

a morning game and an evening game. Both were well attended. The Ardmore independent went 75-65 in 1950 for a first-place finish before 44,454 fans, the highest attendance in Ardmore baseball history. Warren guided the Indians past Ada's talent-packed Herefords in the first round of the playoffs before losing the finals to McAlester's Rockets who were staffed by several future New York Yankees. Warren was named manager of the All-Star team. Nodar led the team in batting with .349, Warren at .303 stroked twenty-one home runs, and John Wilson drove in 118 runs including nineteen home runs.

1951

With the Korean Conflict putting men in uniform, Ardmore had "draft insurance" in its connection with the Cambria pipeline and owner Willingham's connections on the island. A dozen Cubans were under contract when spring training began; nine of them made the team. Six were back from 1950. In terms of talent, this was the best team Ardmore fielded since the 1923 Snappers and 1925 Boomers of the Western Association.

Each Cuban player had a very good 1951 season. With them and the rest of the club, the nine dominated the Sooner State. The team averaged 9.2 runs per game. The Indians led the League in seven categories —a .300 average, 1,289 runs, 1,475 hits, 2,115 total bases, 291 doubles, 1,107 walks and 1,073 RBIs. With 768, they struck out fewer times than any other club. At .950, the 1951 Indians had the best gloves of any Ardmore team. The pitching staff led with 1,062 strike outs, 104 complete games, and gave up only 600 walks, the League's fewest. The ERA was fourth at 4.24, and runs-per-game average was 5.3 but the batters gave the pitchers an average margin of nearly four runs. Armin Somonte, All-Star left hander, was 24-11 with a 2.82 ERA, a League record 341 strike outs and five shut outs to his credit including his second no-hitter, a 18-0 thrashing of Lawton on August 8. Harold Warren, Bennie's nephew, was 22-5 completing twenty-five games and giving up only 3.51 earned runs per nine innings. All-Star outfielder Joe Nodar hit .328 while Havana native and fellow Cuban Ernesto Klein hit .301. Bennie Warren's .354 with twenty-two home runs plus his .991 average behind the plate with no passed balls in 101 games landed him a spot on the All-Star team. Rookie second sacker Manuel Temes earned an All-Star spot by tying for the League lead with 195 hits and 155 RBIs and averaging .340 at the plate. The Indians won the regular season pennant going away with a 99-40 record and a winning percentage of .712. After eliminating Pauls Valley in a three game sweep, the Indians could not shake the McAlester hex losing the finals to the fourth-place Rockets four games to two. Four Indians were named to the All-Star team, Warren as catcher and Cubans at second base, center field, and on the mound. Attendance, however, slipped to 40,742.

In 1951, the Ardmore business community sold $1,475 worth of ticket books, the fans raised

With seven Cubans, the 1951 Ardmore Indians won the regular season setting a League record for wins. L-R Top row: Orel Dryden, Jack Rose, Lloyd Stout, Darrell Pierce, Glen Groomes, Ernesto Klein, Craig Whitstone, Glenn Snyder, manager Bennie Warren, owner Arthur Willingham, announcer Puny Sparger, and Maurice Bridge. Front row: Harold Warren, Jack Fuller, Osmaro Blanco, Joe Nodar, Hector Bonet, Armin Somonte, Manuel Caldaso, and Manuel Temes.

$1,650 for the players' fund, and Waco Turner handed out $1,800 in cash performance bonuses to players. Success on the field and at the gate did not overcome the glaring defect in the franchise: Tribe Park.   When Art Willingham acquired the franchise in 1950, he also leased Tribe Park and had a sublease on the ground. After two seasons, Willingham cited the strain of commuting between Sherman and Ardmore as a reason to sell the team. At the annual League meeting in November, 1951, Willingham summarized the facility: the lighting is mediocre, the playing field is fair, and the stands are deplorable. He delivered an ultimatum to the citizens of Ardmore: provide a new ball park or he would move the team. When the voters turned down a $75,000 bond issue by seventy-three votes of 2,100 cast —Oklahoma requires a sixty percent vote— in the December, 1951 election, the fate of Ardmore baseball, at least in the current incarnation, was sealed. Willingham was good to his word: the Indians moved. Sherman, Texas, had become an open territory when Arturo Gonzalez moved his Class B Twins to Paris after the 1951 season. At the January, 1952 League meeting, Willingham was granted approval to move his franchise to his hometown. Ardmore was without professional baseball.

1952

While Ardmore was winning the 1951 crown, "Ironman" Fred McDuff and his Seminole club were suffering through one of the worst seasons any Sooner State League team had experienced. The self-proclaimed king of oil field equipment dealers, sporting his signature red carnation, McDuff had saved baseball in Seminole in August, 1950, by purchasing the Oilers as they tottered on insolvency. For some $11,000 he got the franchise lock, stock, and barrel together with the right to name it, which he did. The Oilers became "McDuff's Seminole Ironmen." He may have had an eye for used oil-field iron but his view of baseball was myopic. To build a core of players, he signed many of the 1950 semi-pro champion Elk City Elks along with their playing manager, Dwight "Rip" Collins, as well as a number castaways from the Class D ranks.

After a particularly awful twelve-game road trip on which he had accompanied the team, McDuff fired Collins, released five players, and appointed a veteran outfielder, Bill Stumborg, to guide the club. When that didn't work, he released an injured Stumborg and signed Dutch Prather to lead the unruly charges. McDuff was quoted in the June 27, 1951, issue of *The Sporting News* that the team was for sale. "It is just too expensive" he said but "I've bowed my neck and we will go through the season." With Len Gilmore on the mound for both ends of a doubleheader with Shawnee on the last day of the campaign, McDuff remarked "We bowed out in a blaze of glory, and I hope Seminole has a team next year."

On December 27, the front page news in Seminole was a pending sale of the franchise, nine player contracts, and options on equipment and a bus to Hayden Bryce, manager of the local Mistletoe Express office. As things unfolded, Bryce was betting on the come. His plan was to set up a non-profit entity, assemble an executive committee, and solicit donations. McDuff told the *Seminole Producer* "I hope that [Bryce] profits by my experience with the team –take account of what I've done

The Ironman, Fred McDuff.

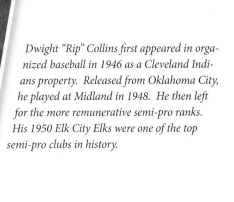

Dwight "Rip" Collins first appeared in organized baseball in 1946 as a Cleveland Indians property. Released from Oklahoma City, he played at Midland in 1948. He then left for the more remunerative semi-pro ranks. His 1950 Elk City Elks were one of the top semi-pro clubs in history.

and stay away from that." He promptly withdrew his guaranty deposit from the National Association. Bryce could not come up with the financial wherewithal to swing the purchase. Former Oilers manager Hugh Willingham lined up a working agreement with Detroit as the local American Legion scrambled to raise $10,000 to keep the team. Despite these efforts and after a ten-day extension from a previous January 14 deadline, the franchise reverted to the League.

Duncan, Gainesville and Paris, Texas, as well as Ardmore —two weeks after Art Willingham moved the Indians to Sherman, Texas—were bidding for the right to join or re-join the League. A trio of Ardmore business and professional men, jeweler W. C. Peden, attorney Lester Cooke, and American Legion executive and machine shop operator A. P. "Pink" Shuman, appeared before a committee of League owners in Sherman. Based on their promise to build a $75,000 ball park before the 1953 season, Ardmore landed the franchise by four votes to three. The League approved the move on January 27, 1952. The worst team in Seminole's history was about to become the worst Ardmore ever fielded.

The new Ardmore Indians started with less than McDuff did. None of the 1951 Ironmen appeared on the Ardmore roster; the most talented of those had signed with Shawnee. In fact, the only player from the 1951 Indians to play at Tribe Park in 1952 was Havana's Ernesto Klein whom independent Vernon, Texas, returned after forty-six games. Five-year old Tribe Park was run down and deserved all the criticism the past tenant, Art Willingham, heaped on it. The Cuban connection was cut off with the new Sherman Twins assuming Ardmore's place in the Cambria queue.

Carl "Jackie" Sullivan, a hot-tempered second baseman who consistently hit over .300 in Class D, was hired to assemble a club as a non-playing man-

Jackie Sullivan got into one game with the wartime Detroit Tigers on July 6, 1944. He handled his only attempt in the field. He joined the West Texas-New Mexico League where he led Lubbock, Lamesa, and Plainview.

ager. Of the thirty-one who appeared for the 1952 Indians, ten were rookies who never got through the season or were discards from another Class D team. For five more, Ardmore was where their careers ended. Only one player, rookie Glen Crable with a 13-14 record and 4.39 ERA, made it to the AAA level. Only three of the 1952 Indians played any part of the 1956 season in Organized Baseball.

The 1952 season was plagued from the start. Joe Nodar had run a tryout camp in Havana and sent the Indians seven players. Sullivan scouted all over north Texas and picked the best he could find from a tryout camp at Farmersville. The Cubans and the rookie cowboys with veterans Sullivan and Royce Mills formed the 1952 Indians. Twenty-two pitchers appeared in fewer than twenty-seven innings. Fourteen position players saw action in fewer than ten games. The team went from first in 1951 to last in every category in 1952. The club's .245 batting average complimented having the fewest hits, runs, total bases, triples, RBIs and the most strike outs. With 430 errors, the 1952 team's .923 fielding average bested the ball-bobbling 1950 Indians for the worst.

Sullivan was fined $25 for arguing with an umpire on April 30. He quit in a pique May 2 when the team would not break League rules and pay it. Veteran pitcher Mills, who came over from Lubbock with Sullivan, served in the dugout for three days until Hugh Willingham could trade his deputy sheriff's uniform for Ardmore flannels. He gave up on July 8. In this third season, limited service pitcher Clyde Baldwin took over for a week then went on the disabled list. Pitcher Julian Morgan, who had been in Organized Ball since 1938, became the fifth field leader on July 13.

On the field, Charlie Rabe of Lawton had Ardmore's number. He threw eighteen consecutive hitless, scoreless innings against them on June 20 and June 24. The first nine innings were in relief.

Rabe had no wins against four losses in the National League.

The second was a 2-0 gem. Bennie Warren, now at the helm of Sherman, gave his old club a remembrance on August 31, when he hit a grand slam out of Tribe Park.

The fans responded by staying away. Attendance dropped to 24,362 from 40,742 the previous year. W.C. Peden, president of the club, announced that the team was for sale after finishing the 1952 season $5,000 in the red. The Ardmore Chamber of Commerce launched a campaign to raise $20,000.

The franchise lacked the cash for train or even bus tickets for the 1952 Indians who finished the season. In a post-season exhibition to raise money to send the players home, Ardmore won the "Booby Bowl" 5-4 in eleven innings against the Blackwell Broncos, fifth-place finisher in the K-O-M League's final season.

Baseball-starved Blackwell, Oklahoma, landed the Carthage, Missouri, K-O-M franchise in 1952, and responded to the Broncos with 51,000 paid admissions. They played against Ardmore in the only post-season contest ever between a K-O-M club and a Sooner State League team. That turned out to be the last game a K-O-M League team ever played in. The Class D circuit folded after the 1952 playoffs

1953-1957 CARDINAL YEARS

SEASON	ATTENDANCE	RECORD	FINISH	AFFILIATION	PLAYOFF FIRST ROUND	PLAYOFF FINALS
1953	43,000	91-46	First	St. Louis (NL)	Lost to McAlester 1-3	
1954	31,090	72-67	Fourth	St. Louis	Beat Shawnee 3-2	Lost to Lawton 0-4
1955	33,731	65-75	Fifth	St. Louis		
1956	47,110	83-56	First	St. Louis	Beat Paris 3-2	Lost to Seminole 3-4
1957	36,301	74-52	Second	St. Louis	Beat Muskogee 3-0	Beat Paris 4-0

CHAPTER TWO   1953

Peden called a public meeting for November 13, 1952, to decide the fate of baseball in Ardmore. Oil millionaire Waco Turner came to the rescue bringing an entrepreneur's energy and acumen and, of most immediate need, money. He became president of Ardmore Baseball Association and immediately began a search for a working agreement. He hired *The Daily Ardmoreite* city editor Bill Hamilton to serve as business manager and become his sports captain. Quickly Ardmore became the seventh Class D team in the St. Louis

Cardinals' farm system and with that a stream of good players flowed south. The word at the Cardinals' Albany, Georgia, spring camp was that a player wanted to be on Waco's team. Turner's wife, Opie, set up a lucrative bonus system. Bennie Warren, who led the 1951 Indians to the best Ardmore record ever and the playoff finals, was hired away from the Willingham organization. The team began the season as the Indians. After Waco Turner jawboned the St. Louis front office for new uniforms identical to the National League club the Indians became Cardinals. The 1953 team responded with one of the best records in Ardmore baseball history and the highest attendance to date, 43,000.

When Waco Turner succeeded W.C. Peden as president of the ball club in the fall of 1952, he accelerated planned improvements to Tribe Park to put the facility in condition for an April 6, 1953, exhibition game between the St. Louis Browns and the Chicago Cubs who were returning together from spring training in California. He doubled the capacity by adding new boxes at field level, extended the grandstand, added bleachers on both ends, built concrete dugouts, quadrupled the size of the press box, and built two new clubhouses for the players. Turner moved his crews from the golf course at Dornick Hills Country Club to put the playing surface in its best condition ever. When

Bleachers, left and below left, and field boxes below.

an inch of rain fell the evening before the exhibition, Turner had a tank truck driven to the field. A drilling crew soaked the infield dirt with dozens of barrels of gasoline and then lit it. The infield was baked dry for the Major Leaguers.

Two of the hapless 1952 Indians appeared for the 1953 Cardinals, light hitting Bob Folkert, who

retired after the season, and Glen Crable who was at 13-14 the best hurler of 1952; he was 17-13 in 1953. Tom Anderson, who played semi-pro ball for Marietta, Oklahoma, in 1952, came back to Ardmore with the club from spring training in Albany, Georgia, but was released the day before the season began; Ardmore had a surplus of outfielders. Anderson

Improvements made by Waco Turner included dugouts, press box, club house, field boxes, and bleachers.

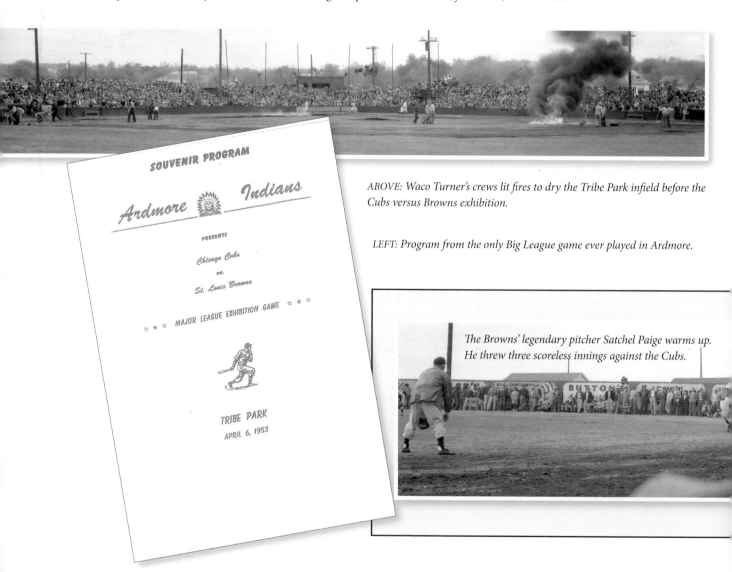

ABOVE: *Waco Turner's crews lit fires to dry the Tribe Park infield before the Cubs versus Browns exhibition.*

LEFT: *Program from the only Big League game ever played in Ardmore.*

SOUVENIR PROGRAM

Ardmore Indians

PRESENTS

Chicago Cubs

vs.

St. Louis Browns

☆ ☆ ☆ MAJOR LEAGUE EXHIBITION GAME ☆ ☆ ☆

TRIBE PARK
APRIL 6, 1953

The Browns' legendary pitcher Satchel Paige warms up. He threw three scoreless innings against the Cubs.

remained as the team's bus driver and trainer for five seasons. Future Major Leaguers Jackie Brandt, Bob Blaylock, and Marty Kutyna toiled for the Cardinals' 1953 farm club. At .270 they tied with Ada for the highest team average and outscored opponents 1,004 to 763. Al Viotta's .385 batting average was good enough only for second place in the League competition behind McAlester's Russ Snyder's Silver Bat winning .432, the best in all the Minors. The pitching staff's collective 4.38 ERA

The 1953 Ardmore Indians on July 11, 1953 with Waco (white hat) and Opie Turner in the top row. When new uniforms arrived from St. Louis toward the end of the season, they became the Cardinals.

Ageless Satchel Paige played his last Major League season with the 1953 St. Louis Browns. When the charter train carrying the Browns and Cubs pulled into Ardmore, all the players were escorted to the Hotel Ardmore for a luncheon and a little pre-game glad-handing. All, that is, except Satchel Paige, the only African-American on either squad. Jim Crow was the law and custom in Oklahoma and Ardmore was no exception. Paige was escorted east from the train station by the Ardmore Colored Chamber of Commerce, which had purchased five hundred tickets for the game, for his rest before starting the afternoon contest.

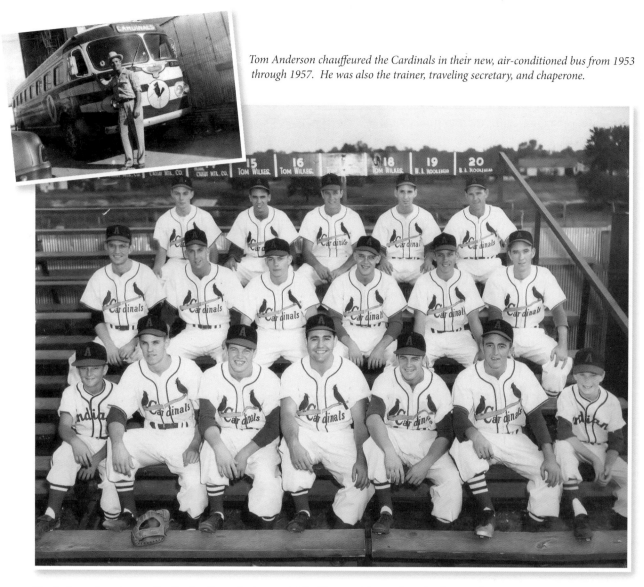

Tom Anderson chauffeured the Cardinals in their new, air-conditioned bus from 1953 through 1957. He was also the trainer, traveling secretary, and chaperone.

The Ardmore team in new Cardinal uniforms in August, 1953. They would wear these for the next four seasons. The top row of Tribe Park was the reserved seating. The names below the numbers identify the holders.

was balanced but not outstanding. Fielding at .939 was good enough for fifth. In the most important category, however, at 91-46 the Indians finished the campaign six games up on Shawnee. A competitive pennant race that Ardmore won put attendance up by nearly 20,000 over 1952.

Jim Farmer tied the League record for walks on May 27 with twenty-one; coupled with ten Shawnee hits, he dropped the decision 22-4. Blaylock, a

seventeen-year old who joined the club in June fresh from Muldrow, Oklahoma, High School, recovered from being hit in the face by a line drive off the bat of Sherman-Denison's Van Anthony on July 9, to finish the season 9-1 with a 3.48 ERA. Outfielder Al Viotta exacted some revenge near the end of the season when he sent Anthony to the hospital for facial stitches while stealing home. Ardmore won a protest of the July 31 game McAlester had won on the field when rookie catcher Don Saatzer conferred with Rockets' manager Bill Cope who was sitting in the box seats because of an indefinite suspension he had earned for shoving an umpire the previous game.

On August 5, rookie Roy "Peanuts" Moore treated the home town fans to a no-hitter against Sherman-Denison. He pitched around five errors but lost the shut out when he gave up seven walks to let three Twins cross the plate in the ninth inning for a 7-3 Indians victory.

Rookie Jackie Brandt, who received a $150 signing bonus and $200 per month, was hitting .342 at mid-season earning a place on the All-Star team along with manager Warren and Viotta, who led the League in runs and RBIs. McAlester extended its playoff *gris gris* against Ardmore, eliminating the Cardinals in the first round.

1954

Bennie Warren was back at the helm as the 1954 season began. Things got off to a rough start on the field. Nature rained out five games. Manager Warren and pitcher Peanuts Moore were ejected for arguing on May 3; Moore with a sore arm was soon released and finished his career with Pauls Valley. The home team won 6-5. In the same game, umpire Leo Hanning cleared the Ardmore bench in the seventh inning for heckling. Late May was particularly rough. Bucking League rules, Waco Turner ordered that ticket price be dropped a third to 50¢ after attendance lagged. With the Cardinals in seventh place and not yet having won twenty games, the parent Cardinals fired Warren on June 15, and brought in Frank Mancuso.

Meridian, Mississippi's Roy "Peanuts" Moore at spring training 1953. He tossed Ardmore's fifth and final no-hitter since the first by Nick Carter in 1921.

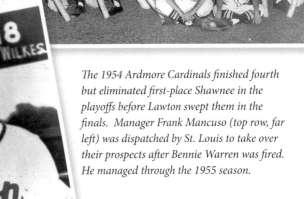

The 1954 Ardmore Cardinals finished fourth but eliminated first-place Shawnee in the playoffs before Lawton swept them in the finals. Manager Frank Mancuso (top row, far left) was dispatched by St. Louis to take over their prospects after Bennie Warren was fired. He managed through the 1955 season.

Derril McGuire was one of the Cardinals' batboys. Waco Turner paid them $2.50 whenever Ardmore won. On the road, he would share a room with Tom Anderson. It was feared the players might be a bad influence.

All-Star and future Major Leaguer Gene Green hit five of his thirty-four home runs against Shawnee on July 15 and July 16 driving in seven runs. By August 5, the Cardinals had only climbed to sixth place at 50-57. A week later they had passed Ada for fifth at 55-59. By season end, the 72-67 Cardinals had edged out the 72-68 Gainesville Owls by one-half game for fourth place. President Clanton ordered that Lawton and Ardmore play a rained out game because the Owls had played one more game. National Association president George Trautman overruled Clanton and declared Ardmore was the sole occupant of fourth and in the playoff. A game must be made up only if there is a tie for fourth place.

In the first round, the Cardinals whipped Shawnee, regular season winner by ten and one-half games, but were swept in the finals by Lawton in the little Braves' first year working with Milwaukee.

Waco Turner's administrative assistant, Beth Jones, worked overtime selling tickets at Cardinals' home games. Turner's right hand man, trainer, bus driver, and crew boss, Tom Anderson, looks on. The ticket prices had been cut to 50¢ when this photo was taken.

Wedding applause and an eighteen bat salute for Mr. and Mrs. Chuck Staniland as they pass from home plate to the pitcher's mound on July 7, 1954.

There was even a Miss Ardmore Cardinal.

Jewelers continued providing end-of-season awards in 1954. L-R: Manager Frank Mancuso, Ida Barnett of Long's Jewelers, W.C.Peden, Tom Anderson, Maurice Bridge, board member Charles Goddard, Gene Green, the outstanding batter, John Gerace, the outstanding pitcher, and Bob White, most popular player. Front: batboys Bobby Williams and Derril McGuire. Goddard holds the award for the highest opening day attendance and the Governor's Cup. The team bought Mancuso leather luggage and spikes for the batboys. Strasmick's Jewelers donated the trophies for Green and Gerace. White received a $100 watch from Long's Jewelers.

A team batting average of .285 along with leading the League with 2,337 total bases and 191 home runs were only good enough to place third in hitting during the 1954 season. Shawnee ran away with the pennant. The Ardmore bats were good enough to make up for the shabby fielding —.932 with 354 errors— and second division 5.37 ERA pitching. The pitching staff led the League only in balks.

As 1954 attendance tumbled to 31,090, club president Waco Turner announced the team's demise. As close acquaintances of Turner repeated, baseball would be a big hit in Ardmore or Waco would not be in the game long; he had no use for a lemon. The board of directors voted to close down the franchise as of October 1. Turner returned the working agreement for the 1955 season and cancelled the planned exhibition between St. Louis and the Chicago White Sox on April 5, 1955.

1955

Something happened in the next two weeks; perhaps Turner called on St. Louis owner Augustus Busch. In any event, the working agreement was revived and the Ardmore Cardinals were good to go for 1955. The cancellation of the exhibition stood.

Frank Mancuso was re-hired. St. Louis, however, sent down a second division club. Fifth in the final standings, the Cardinals' .241 was sixth in batting despite 115 home runs, seventh in pitching with a team 4.57 ERA, and barely third in fielding at .943. Mike O'Conner set a then-League record for strike outs in a nine-inning game: twenty-one on July 1 against Ponca City. By identical scores of 2-1, the Cardinals swept Shawnee on May 25. Idabel, Oklahoma, native Charlie Purtle got his

The Cardinals' board of directors met in the club's office in the basement of the Hotel Ardmore on September 29, 1954, to decide the team's fate. Board members were Quinton Little, Leon Daube, Charles Goddard, Bill Hamilton, and Waco Turner. Woodrow Hulme was auditor and Shirley Patterson served as secretary.

twentieth win August 19, despite giving up fourteen hits, 9-7 over Ponca City. He had been deprived of a no-hitter earlier in the season when McAlester stroked a single in the top of the ninth inning. Roger Cook threw a one-hitter against McAlester on August 26, winning 6-0. With Seminole leading 5-3, an eighth-inning Mancuso rhubarb with plate umpire Leo Hanning resulted in a forfeiture on September 1. The Cardinals lost big in the last game of the season 28-5. Bob Dennis, Lawton third baseman, had seven hits, eighteen total bases and twelve RBIs on the way to setting three all-time League records.

Only 33,731 Ardmoreites passed through the gates at Boundary and Washington Street in 1955. Perhaps the poor attendance was a sign of bad karma resulting from a fan stealing Paris catcher Rob Sternper's glove and $25 from the visitor's dugout on May 6. Maybe it was the fifth-place finish thirty and one-half games out. Whatever it was, Waco Turner walked away. New management led by A.P. "Pink" Shuman, who was promptly elected to the League's board of control, re-signed with St. Louis.

Talk of a new ball park came with each season. A one-year extension of the ground lease was obtained for the 1955 season. After that campaign, the Ardmore School Board, which had become the landowner, made the ballclub's decision about looking for a new home field for the Cardinals when they decided to build Will Rogers Elementary School on the site of Tribe Park.

1956

Waco Turner had expended a huge amount of energy and treasure to take Dornick Hills Country Club from a bankrupt, poorly maintained links to the host of a regular stop on the PGA tour. A turf fight on the country club's board and his expulsion as both president and a member caused him to figuratively kick the dust of Ardmore off his boots. He had begun building his own country club, Burneyville golf resort, in late 1955.

Occupied with golf, he relinquished the presidency of the ball club to Shuman in December, 1955. Austin Smith, Felix Simmons, and Earle Garrison joined him as officers. C. P. Sebastian was hired as business manager and would remain in that role through the 1961 season of the Rosebuds. The next month the Community Youth Foundation broke ground on property Shuman had located and Turner, Leon Daube, and Ward Merrick had purchased for the long hoped new ball park. To be named Cardinal Park, the 1,800 capacity facility would cost $80,000 and be ready for the 1956 season. The press box, clubhouses and lighting were moved to the new facility as the demolition of Tribe Park proceeded into early 1956. The stanchions for the lights were replaced by oil derricks. The fences were short: 310 feet to left, 371 feet to center and 320 feet down the right field line. It was, like Tribe Park, roofless.

Oklahoma Governor Raymond Gary and League president George Barr were in attendance to celebrate the new ball park when the Cardinals and Lawton played the first game there on April 24, 1956. The Braves ruined Ardmore's debut at home blanking the Redbirds 5-0 on four hits. With the capacity expanded to 2,800, it was the home of the Ardmore Rosebuds of the Texas League from June 4, 1961, until the season's end. Since then the stands have been removed and replaced with small bleachers. A few junior high school games are played there today.

The 1955 Ardmore Cardinals.

Cardinal Park is unique in having lighting towers made from oil derricks. 2008 photo.

The parent Cardinals reached into the lower levels of its farm system for the last manager of the Ardmore club, J.C. Dunn. At age thirty, he had been a successful teacher of the game as well as a hard hitting Class D first baseman. Dunn's 1956 charges got off to a slow start, languishing in the second division the first month of the season. Mental lapses plagued the young players. Jim Bradley, who was a rookie at McAlester in 1952, lost a home run on June 8, when he failed to touch home plate. Gene Oliver, who would begin a ten-year Major League career in 1959, knocked one out of Cardinal Park on June 20, with a man on first. That man was manager Dunn who was holding to see whether the ball would clear the fence. Oliver was supremely confident and ran past Dunn. Dunn was still on first while Oliver was called out and credited with a single.

Then the Redbirds charged, led by Bobby Stangel's fifteen-game hitting streak and thirty-seven stolen bases and Dick Wodka's ten wins, to take over first place by mid-season. They never looked back to finish three and one-half games ahead of Lawton with an 83-56 record. Regular season attendance jumped to 47,110, 56,052 counting the playoffs.

Dunn hit for the cycle on August 6, driving in seven runs while Oliver had a home run, double, and two singles and six RBIs to crush second-place Lawton 22-5. At Appreciation Night on September 1, the fans presented Dunn with $1,000 and the team reciprocated with Gene Oliver hitting his thirty-ninth home run, tying a League record, and John Bartek becoming the only twenty-game winner in the League as they clinched the pennant with a 5-3 win over Lawton. It was like the good old days of

Bennie Warren's Indians.

Ardmore led the League in most hitting categories —runs, hits, total bases, doubles, home runs, and RBIs— despite a .273 team average, middling most years but the best in a well-balanced League in 1956. It was a good fielding team with a .9427 average and errors per game down to a manageable 2.2. The Cardinals should attribute their regular season finish by three and one-half games over Lawton to their 16-3 regular season dominance over McAlester.

Three of the top ten hitters were members of the Cardinals. Phil Jantze hit .343, Dunn .336, and Oliver .334. Pitchers John Bartek finished 21-6, Wodka 15-9, Turk 15-9, and Vince "the Finn" Kipela 14-9. The staff ERA was 4.39. Aviotti, Jantze, Oliver, and Bartek were named to the All-Star team.

Vince Kipela led the League with 276 strike outs and set a League fielding record with no errors in 231 innings, a perfect 1.000.

McAlester was a New York Yankees farm club. The 1956 team was the last edition of the Rockets finishing seventh in the Sooner State League race.

The 1956 Ardmore Cardinals won the regular season but dropped the playoffs to the "Miracle" Seminole Oilers in seven games. L-R: Top row: Jim Henric, John Bartek, Walt Matthews, Gene Oliver, manager J. C. Dunn, Larry Riggs, Phil Jantze, Jim Turk, and Dick Wodka. Front row: Ron Voyles, Ron Ott, Pete Aviotti, Bob Stangel, Vince Kipela, Curt Jantze, Jim Bradley, and Tom Fassler. Batboys: Ray Filippi (left) and John Saunders. A taller Saunders would also serve as the batboy for the Ardmore Rosebuds in 1961.

The Cardinals edged a strong fourth-place Paris team to reach the 1956 finals against Seminole. Burl Storie's light-hitting but hard throwing Oilers —the team's batting average was .248, ERA was 4.23— came from last place in July to finish third. They were not to be denied. They put away Ardmore 16-5 in the seventh game on September 16, to win the only championship for that franchise and the second flag for the city of Seminole.

1957

J.C. Dunn was back at the helm for the shortened 126-game 1957 season. Teams were allowed sixteen members with two veterans, up to six limited service players, and at least eight rookies. The season had been shortened to avoid the rain that had plagued the early weeks of the past two seasons. On May 1, three of four openers, including the game at Ardmore, were rained out.

The Cardinals jumped into second place on May 9, when they snapped newcomer Greenville's six-game opening winning streak, and then went on to win five in a row before Shawnee's Hawks knocked the Cardinals from the air 7-4 on May 12. On May 15, St. Louis native and starter Tom Fassler drove in five runs with a triple and a single before being relieved in the sixth. Reliever John McFadden added two singles and two RBIs to save Fassler's first win 14-2 over Lawton. Four errors and nine hits in the fourth inning gave Shawnee a 15-4 win over the Cardinals on May 19. Left hander Don Mitchell threw eighteen scoreless innings before Seminole tagged him for four runs on May 21; he managed to hold on for an 11-4 win putting Ardmore in first place. In his next start on May 27, he dropped a twelve-inning match to Muskogee. The next day,

A.P. Shuman and J.C. Dunn before the Ardmore Cardinals traveled to the 1957 season opener at Lawton. 1961 would be the last season for both.

Fassler gave up four runs in the first inning. Dunn sent Bill Dikeman to warm up. Dunn went to the mound a couple of times to make more time for his reliever to get loose. The umpire accused him of delaying the game. Dunn characteristically disagreed. The result was a 9-0 loss to Muskogee on a forfeit and a tumble to second behind the little Giants.

Ardmore's mastery over Yankee farm teams came to an end on June 20, when Greenville hit past the Cardinals 6-1. McAlester had dropped thirty-six straight in Tribe Park and Cardinal Park since 1953. The Majors had lost the first two there in 1957. After that Ardmore caught fire. Winning five of six from second-place Muskogee in a July 17-21 series and scoring sixty-six runs, the Cardinals went to 54-26, ten games ahead of the pack. The Giants trailed 44-36, a half game ahead of Paris at 43-36. Losing five straight to Greenville, Ardmore's lead was cut to one and one-half games over Paris before rallying to go seven and one-half games up on August 6.

Two nights later, manager Dunn was shot twice by an angry hotel porter who was gunning for center fielder Coy Smith. The night before, Ardmore had lost to the Ponca City Cubs on future

Hall of Famer Billy Williams' walk off single. Returning to the hotel in Ponca City, several of the players procured through the elevator operator or porter the services of a couple of ladies of the night. There was a dispute over terms of payment and the Ardmore players, out-numbering the porter, beat and kicked him. Outfielder and all-star Coy Smith was the ring leader. The porter promised them that "I'll get you." The next evening during the second inning, Dunn was returning to the Cardinals' dugout after scoring. The porter fired several shots intended for Smith, who set out running when he saw him, but hit Dunn. With bullets in his left breast and upper right leg, Dunn went to the hospital and everyone else to the showers; the game was continued the next evening.

With veteran scout and manager Mike Ryba as interim leader, the Redbirds lost seventeen of their last thirty games, including those after Dunn's return on August 22. Ardmore lost five of eight to Lawton with the August 28 loss foreclosing a first-place finish. Paris edged them by one-half game for the regular season pennant.

In the first playoff round, Dunn had two doubles and a single to pace his Cardinals to a 10-4 win over Muskogee. On Appreciation Night at Ardmore, he had four hits including a home run for a come from behind 10-9 win. The sweep was completed with a 5-4 victory at Muskogee.

Paris, the winner over Shawnee, faced Ardmore in the finals. In the first match at Paris, J. C. Dunn broke open the game in the ninth inning with a three-run blast, followed by Jim McKnight's solo homer for an 8-3 win. The Cards won game two 10-5 on Dunn's three RBIs and McFadden's relief. Back in Cardinal Park, the home team clipped the Orioles 10-8 with McKnight's five RBIs and Dunn's

home run. On September 10, Norman Frye, 11-7 during the season, handcuffed Paris on four hits to win 6-1. The championship clincher was Frye's last professional game, the last Ardmore Cardinals game, and the last Sooner State League game.

Statistically the 1957 Ardmore Cardinals team did not look like a champion. While 718 runs and one hundred stolen bases led the League, the team hit only .265. The power that had carried the team in past years was absent in 1957; only eighty-one balls cleared the short League fences. Jim McKnight led the League by batting .341 and driving in 112 runs. The best-fielding Ardmore team since 1951, its .94504 average was only sixth. The pitching staff failed to lead the League in any category and finished barely third with a 4.11 ERA. Keller, 15-6, was the only hurler to finish in the League's top ten with a 3.20 ERA.

The owners agreed to suspend Sooner State League play in 1958 with hope of reconfiguring. As the Minor Leagues consolidated and farm systems shrank, the last Class D league west of the Mississippi quietly disbanded in February, 1959. The baseball organization in Ardmore remained alive with Tom Anderson succeeding C. P. Sebastian as business manager in January, 1958, and Pink Shuman remaining as president. In 1961, their tenacity was rewarded.

John Jeanes, the Paris Orioles' and Sooner State League's top pitcher with a 2.41 ERA, could not halt the Cardinal attack.

37

CHAPTER THREE

1961 SHORT SEASON OF THE ROSEBUDS

Oil and ranching millionaire Tom O'Connor, Jr., tired after three seasons of losing money, sold the Class AA Texas League Victoria, Texas, ballclub to Derrest Williams after the 1960 season. Williams, who had played semi-pro ball and owned and managed at Texas City, had been the general manager of the "Rosebuds." The team was so named because Victoria was known as the "Rose City" on account of the rose garden in Riverside Park (where the ballpark was located), and the Victoria teams in the early part of the century had borne that moniker.

Riverside Park ● Victoria, Texas

Home of the Rosebuds before Ardmore.

Williams scrambled to secure a working agreement after Detroit moved its AA farm elsewhere. On April 4 he told the Victoria Buds Boosters that Ardmore interests had offered $100,000 for him to move the team. Williams said he demurred because he wanted to keep the team in Victoria even though season ticket sales were $20,000 under 1960. The first five weeks of the 1961 season saw attendance at Riverside Park plummet to unsustainable lows. In twenty-four home dates at Victoria, the Rosebuds drew 12,969. Without the 1,664 at the season opener and 1,392 at the swansong on May 26, attendance averaged 314, poor for even a Class D team. Williams, losing $500 per night, obtained permission to quickly move the team to Ardmore, Oklahoma. The 1961 Rosebuds left Victoria for good after winning a 10-3 contest over Tulsa on May 26. The next day the move to Ardmore became official while on a road trip to Amarillo.

On May 27, the Ardmore Baseball Association, which had owned the Class D Cardinals in the Sooner State League, opened for business as operator of the Ardmore Rosebuds. A. P. "Pink" Shuman remained president of the group. Jack Caro, who had begun the season on the Rosebud's roster, followed the franchise to Ardmore as business manager; Williams, who retained ownership of the franchise, remained in Victoria with his beer distributorships. Offices were set up in the lobby of the Hotel Ardmore. Ardmore's population at 21,000 was 50,000 smaller than Victoria.

Except for the 1952 season, Ardmore's Sooner State League teams had drawn between 31,000 and 47,000. To prove that Ardmore could support a higher class of baseball, Shuman arranged for the Houston Buffaloes to play the Tulsa Oilers in a 1958 regular season game. The contest drew an overflow

Closing the transfer of the Rosebuds. Top: C. P. Sebastian, Derrest Williams, Ardmore City Manager. Seated: A. P. Shuman.

3,100 Ardmoreites to Cardinal Park. While by far the smallest city in the Texas League, 1961 Ardmore attendance numbers beat the last place drawing team, Jimmy Humphries' Rio Grande Valley Giants who relocated to Victoria in June. Attendance between Victoria (12,969) and Ardmore (35, 925) would be 48,894.

Ardmore was not a strange place, however, for five players who had spent time in the Sooner State League. Both Dennis Loudenback and Al Owen appeared for the 1956 Ponca City Cubs. Jim "Rube" Melton played his rookie year, 1949, at Pauls

Al Owen began the season with Victoria and made the move to Ardmore. He was hitting .284 when traded into the Chicago White Sox organization. In his last season, 1962, he played third base for the Class AAA Oklahoma City 89ers.

BELOW: Dennis Loudenback slides safely against Austin. At age 24, he retired from baseball after the 1961 season.

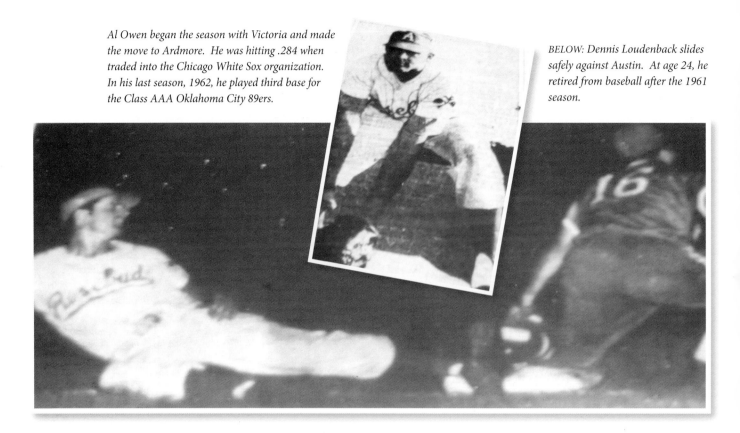

Valley where he was an All-Star with a 23-8 record. Pitcher Marshall Renfroe spent the 1956 and 1957 seasons as a Yankees farmhand at McAlester and Greenville. The 1956 and 1957 Ardmore Cardinals' player-manager, J.C. Dunn, following serving the same role at Dothan of the Alabama-Florida League from 1958 through 1960, had his second look at pitching above the Class B level. Coming in for the last four games of the season after Mickey McGuire was called up to Rochester of the International League, he hung up his spikes after batting .188 with no home runs or RBIs in sixteen at bats.

The Ardmore Rosebuds made their first home appearance at the expanded 2,800-seat Cardinal Park on Sunday, June 4. Under threatening skies, 1,441 watched the Austin Senators top the Rosebuds 5-3 with the wildness of former Senator Mike Marinko accounting for the margin of victory

All was not copacetic, however. Referring to fan complaints about the club preventing bleacher fans who paid 75¢ for a seat moving to the $1.25 grandstand *gratis* and the policy of making fans return foul balls hit into the stands, *The Daily Ardmoreite* sports editor Doyle May wrote "We never thought we'd see the day when Ardmore fans would use such petty excuses to stay away from a game." It was fairly easy to move around Cardinal Park because the bleacher area was nearly indistinguishable from the general admission seats in the grandstand. Only admittance to the box seats was enforced. As to foul balls, nearly every ball that did not land in fair territory landed outside of the park. There were always a dozen or so youths —mostly from the neighborhood— standing in the west parking lot ready to chase fouls and earn a free pass upon return of the errant ball.

The Ardmore Rosebuds played at Cardinal Park. Built in 1956 for $80,000 it was the roofless home of the Class D Ardmore Cardinals for two years and then the transplanted Rosebuds for ten weeks in 1961. The light stanchions are oil derricks, unique in baseball. With the grandstand dismantled, it is still in use by middle school players.

Long suffering manager George Staller. He was rewarded later with several years as a coach with Earl Weaver's championship Baltimore Orioles.

John Stokoe was a Milwaukee Braves property. He posted a 4-3 record in seventy-six innings for the Rosebuds. He was sent down to Class C Eau Claire. He was released after the 1961 season.

The year 1961 saw the Rosebuds affiliated with Baltimore of the American League. The Orioles were unique in 1961 by having working agreements with two Class AA teams, a limited one with Victoria and a full one with the Little Rocker Travelers of the Southern Association. With a long tradition, better facilities, and better travel connections, Little Rock was the favored farm club.

George Staller, who played for fifteen years including twenty-one games with the Athletics in 1943, managed the club. The eighteen team members who came over from Victoria were catchers Jim Carver and Ken Worley, first basemen Clint McCord and Bob Nelson, second baseman Dennis Loudenback, third baseman Charlie Strange, shortstop Mickey McGuire, utility man Al Owen, left fielder Al Nagel, center fielder Bill Parsons, right fielder Jim Fridley, and pitchers Alex Castro, George Gaffney, Don McLeod, Buster Narum, Merlin Nippert, Marshall Renfroe, and John Stokoe.

Following the move, Art Burnett came over from Tulsa and stayed for twenty-nine games before he was sent down to Greenville S.C. in the Sally League and then to finish the season for Monterrey of the Mexican League. Joining the Ardmore squad on June 14 from Little Rock were Pete Ward and John Papa; Worley and three-year Rosebud veteran Parsons were released to make room for the new arrivals. Roger Kudron of the Travelers joined them three weeks later. Bill "Turkey" Thompson came in a trade that sent Jim Fridley to Mobile of the Southern Association on June 22. Atoka's Billy Joe Dasher, a University of Tulsa student, was acquired from Topeka and reported on June 7; he was released on July 1, re-signed August 10, and then sold to Birmingham three days later. Bob Nelson was sent down to Stockton to make room for pitcher Mike Marinko on loan from Austin. Sooner State League veteran Jim "Rube" Melton of Pauls Valley signed as a free agent for a four-game look-see; he did not stick. Veteran Dick Ewin appeared in twenty-three games hitting .196 before the Rosebuds released him. San Antonio sent 1960 Texas League home run champion Duke Ducote on June 22, just one week after he was demoted from AAA Houston. Catcher Frank Zupo was sent down from Rochester on July 20. In August, the Milwaukee Braves reassigned their farm hands John Stokoe to Eau Claire, Wisconsin, of the Northern League and Marinko to Macon, Georgia, of the Southern Association, leaving the Rosebuds short-handed.

Frank Zupo was a bonus baby in whom the Orioles had a large investment and hope that he would succeed All-Star catcher Gus Triandos. He never made it as a Big League hitter. He finished pro ball as a Kansas City A's property with Dallas of the Pacific Coast League.

Four members of the squad had some limited Major League experience: Jim Fridley with Cleveland in 1952, Baltimore in 1954, and Cincinnati in 1958, Bob Nelson with Baltimore 1955 through 1957, Frank Zupo with Baltimore parts of 1958 and 1959, and Marshall Renfroe, a brief stay with San Francisco in 1959. Six more were to spend time in the Majors following their sojourn in Ardmore: Mickey McGuire at Baltimore in 1962 and 1967, Pete Ward with Baltimore during part of 1962, Chicago White Sox 1963 through 1969, and New York Yankees in 1970, John Miller with Baltimore during 1962 and 1963 and again in 1965 through 1967, Buster Narum with Baltimore in 1963 and Washington 1964 through 1967, Merlin Nippert of Mangum, Oklahoma briefly with Boston in 1962, and John Papa Baltimore for parts of 1961 and 1962.

Billy Joe Dasher had two stints with Ardmore before being sold into the Southern Association.

Jim Melton had been an All-Star for his hometown 1949 regular season champion Pauls Valley Raiders in the Sooner State League. His comeback attempt twelve years later failed.

Despite those past and future Big Leaguers, the 1961 Rosebuds must fairly be called a weak team. One reason was staffing. It was the Orioles' second string AA farm club, obliged only to provide a manager and at least five players. In a six team league, they were fifth in batting at .242, fifth in fielding at .962, and last in pitching. The team ERA of 4.39 was nearly a full earned run higher than fifth-place Rio Grande Valley/Victoria. The mound staff pitched the fewest innings, 1,195, and gave up the most hits, 1,248, most runs, 719, most earned runs, 583, most walks, 611, and hit the most batsmen, forty-three. The club produced only eight shut outs. Kudron gave up twenty-two home runs followed by Renfroe with seventeen. The only positive was that no one committed a balk. Bonus baby John Papa fielded 1.000 but had a win-loss percentage of .000 and allowed 17.37 runners per

nine innings. George Gaffney had the only winning percentage above .500, allowed the fewest runners per nine innings with 7.74 but fielded a semi-pro .852. On his way out of Organized Baseball, Renfroe unloaded thirteen wild pitches and led the team with ninety-five walks and fourteen losses. Narum had a staff-best 115 strikeouts. The ace among the pitchers was Alex Castro who posted a record of 10-11, completed ten of sixteen games started, struck out 111, walked only forty-four, and posted a 3.27 ERA although he allowed over eleven runners per game.

The other problem with the team was the revolving door. Twenty-one position players and twelve pitchers appeared for the Ardmore version of the Rosebuds. Of the twenty on the April 16, opening roster at Victoria, eight finished the season at Ardmore. Two of the most effective pitchers, Don

John Papa was another Baltimore bonus baby who couldn't make the grade. He was "good field, no pitch," fast but wild.

Cuban Alex Castro was one of the most popular Rosebuds. He spent 1962 and 1963 with the Orioles' top farm club at Rochester before retiring from Organized Baseball.

ABOVE: On loan from the Giants farm system, Charlie Strange was the only Rosebud on the 1961 All-Star squad. The Dodgers picked up his contract for 1963 and sent him to a "high" A league. He retired after the 1964 season.

McLeod and Merlin Nippert, were on loan from the Braves' and Red Sox' organizations, respectively. Mike Marinko and John Stokoe were also Braves' property. The team's sole All-Star, Charlie Strange, was borrowed from the Giants' organizations, as was pitcher Marshall Renfroe.

Ward led the team with an average of .307 and also had the highest on-base percentage at .374. Al Nagel's twenty home runs helped him to a .433 slugging percentage and a tie with Dennis Loudenback for most home runs and RBIs. Strange led the team with 543 at bats, sixty-seven runs, 152 hits, 211 total bases, and five triples. These statistics are misleading, however, as Strange's on-base percentage was only .273 and slugging percentage .388. The team was lead-footed. The Rosebuds stole only thirteen bases all season; with six, Pete Ward had nearly half.

There were a couple of busts. Art Burnett who had led the Texas League in 1960 with 111 runs managed only eleven in one hundred at bats before he was moved on. Slugger Duke Ducote had lost his mojo hitting only .195 with three home runs before being released in August. For seven players

Al Nagel hit four home runs in the Ardmore Rosebud's first series on the road at Amarillo. After part-time play in Vancouver in 1962, he retired from the game.

Pete Ward had the most successful career of all the Rosebuds.

Duke Ductoe (.195), J.C. Dunn (.188), Dick Ewin (.196), Dennis Loudenback (.267), Clint McCord (.285), George Gaffney (8-7, 3.61), and Jim Melton (0-0), Ardmore was the last professional team they would play for.

While bleak for the most part, there were some exciting times and stellar performances—

• On May 29, Al Nagel hit four home runs in a single game, a feat not seen in the Texas League since 1903.

• The Texas League played an interlocking schedule with the Mexican League in a union called the Pan-American Association with two All-Star games and a post-season championship series that replaced the old Dixie Series with the Southern Association. The Ardmore club left on June 30 for an eighteen-day road trip south of the border. It began inauspiciously when Mexican customs officials refused to let pitchers Alex Castro, a Cuban, and Don McLeod, a Canadian, enter without an American re-entry visa. Things were held up until the United States consulate issued the necessary documents.

• In the ninth inning of the July 11, inter-league game at Monterrey with the Rosebuds leading, the local fans began throwing objects and firecrackers at the Ardmore outfielders. This spread to the rest of the stands. When umpire Hank Stein could not get the crowd to halt the barrage, he forfeited the game to Ardmore. As the team was leaving the stadium, some four thousand angry fans stoned the bus, breaking four windows but causing no injuries. Mexican League President Eduaro Orvanaños formally apologized to Texas League prexy Dick Butler while the owner of the Sultans did likewise to Ardmore's owner.

• The Ardmore fans were not content to forgive and forget. The Mexico City Red Devils ducked

stones thrown at the team bus by the locals on July 26.

• Behind Don McLeod's three-hitter the Rosebuds won the third game of a triple header at Mexico City on July 9. Due to rain outs, two inter-league games between San Antonio and the Mexico City Red Devils were made up followed by the scheduled match between the Mexico City Tigers and the Rosebuds. Ardmore played the first game of another triple header on July 15, losing to the Red Devils. The next day, McLeod threw a one-hitter at Mexican League leader Veracruz.

• Relief catcher Jim Carver hit the Rosebuds' first and only grand slam at Cardinal Park on July 27, against Poza Rica.

• The Ardmore nine was 16-8 against Mexican League competition. The best series record Ardmore had against a Texas League team was 10-13 versus fifth-place Rio Grande Valley/Victoria.

• The Rosebuds' longest win streak, six games, ended on July 23 with a loss to the Monterrey Sultans.

Carver had the misfortune to be playing behind bonus baby Frank Zupo and the Orioles' regular catcher, All Star Gus Triandos. After a poor start at Charlotte in 1962, he received his release.

• The dugouts emptied in a battle royal after pitcher Marshall Renfroe, frustrated by successive Tulsa homers, decked future Cardinal Mike Shannon at Texas League Park on August 21, en route to a 4-0 loss on Paul Toth's near no-hitter.

• A. P. "Pink" Shuman, long time American Legion baseball leader, an officer of the Sooner State League Cardinals, and Ardmore club president, became ill in July and resigned. He was honored before 1,384 at Cardinal Park on August 10.

Needing to focus on his interests in the Corpus Christi-Victoria area, Derrest Williams advised the League on July 30 that he wished to sell the franchise. By August 10, due to injuries and trades, Ardmore was reduced to a sixteen man roster from the normal twenty-one. That same day Rosebuds' batboy, John Saunders, took ten stitches in the forehead following being struck by a broken bat. The Rosebuds finished the season with a 57-83 record in sixth place thirty-three games behind the champion Amarillo Gold Sox. The Rosebuds ended the season with thirteen loses to only three wins the last two weeks of August. The team was just going through the motions. The Rosebuds lost their last game played in Ardmore to Victoria 20-3 on August 30. They finished the season, fittingly, in Victoria on September 1 with a 2-1 loss despite Buster Narum limiting the Giants to four hits, two of which, unfortunately, were home runs.

The two complaints about Ardmore were Cardinal Park — too small and the field poorly maintained— and its small population. The owners of Tulsa and San Antonio wanted larger cities in the league. Albuquerque and El Paso were both open. Despite reports in *The Sporting News* that Waco and Opie Turner were again coming to the rescue of baseball in Ardmore, they could not come to terms with Williams. Ardmore Baseball Association quickly raised $10,000 for work on the playing surface. But the fix was in. On October 12, the Rosebuds were sold to Duke City Baseball, Inc. and became the Albuquerque Dukes. A bitter Doyle May later wrote a column "Ardmore Never had a Chance." That was a matter of fact.

Ardmore, the smallest city to have AA Texas League baseball, has been without professional baseball since. And with the departure of the Rosebuds, Minor League baseball outside Oklahoma City and Tulsa passed from Oklahoma. It is not without irony that small town Organized Baseball in Oklahoma ended with a last place team in the same league and same town where it began in 1904.

On his way out after a rough game, Marshall Renfroe, like Charlie Strange, was on loan from the Giants. After a 9-14 season at Ardmore, he found himself in the expansion Mets' minor league organization. He hung up his spikes then with a 60-88 lifetime record and one start, two innings, and six runs at the end of the 1959 season with the San Francisco Giants.

Doyle May began his career as a copy writer in Denison, Texas. At age 18, he was the youngest business manager in Organized Baseball with Arturo Gonzalez's Chickasha Chicks in the 1952 Sooner State League. Before becoming sports editor for The Daily Ardmoreite, *he wrote for the Duncan Banner. He retired as sports editors of the Oklahoma Journal.*

CHAPTER FOUR

POST-WAR MAJOR LEAGUERS ARDMORE MAY CLAIM

The Ardmore teams between 1904 and 1926 sent up forty-five players and one umpire to the Major Leagues from short-timers for a cup of coffee like Slats Wilson who got into one game for Washington in 1914, Tom Lovelace, who went to bat for Pittsburgh once in 1922, and Jim Lyle who threw in the Washington Senators' last game of 1925, to Hall of Famer Carl Hubbell, 1927 American League ERA leader and World Series victor Wilcy Moore, to Randy Moore who spent ten seasons in the Show. There were the same number of Major League roster positions then, four hundred, as in the post-War era but fewer leagues and no farm systems within which talent was warehoused under the tyranny of the Reserve Clause. Also, the players were hungrier.

One Indian and eight Cardinals made it to the top, while three already had been there. Bill Upton saw a few innings of action for the 1954 Philadelphia Athletics while Gene Oliver spent ten seasons in the Majors and Chris Cannizzaro was an All-Star catcher. Six members of the Rosebuds reached the top rung but only Pete Ward, Buster Narum, and John Miller played more than a few innings.

BILL UPTON

1948 ARDMORE INDIANS.

Originally signed by the Browns, he was wild in his few starts as a member of the Ada Herefords and released. Ardmore picked up his contract and he joined the Cleveland organization. Before spring training in 1954, the Indians traded him to Philadelphia. Upton saw action as a reliever in two games for the Athletics, giving up one run in five innings. He was sent down to Ottawa on May 3 never to return. His last season was 1957. In his retirement, he taught a number of Los Angeles Dodgers pitchers how to throw a "fork ball."

MITCH CHETKOVICH

1950 ARDMORE INDIANS.

Beginning the 1945 season with the cellar-dwelling Philadelphia Phillies *cum* Blue Jays, he pitched three innings of relief in four games giving up two hits and no runs between April 19 and May 6.

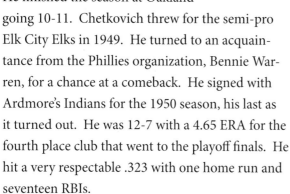

He finished the season at Oakland going 10-11. Chetkovich threw for the semi-pro Elk City Elks in 1949. He turned to an acquaintance from the Phillies organization, Bennie Warren, for a chance at a comeback. He signed with Ardmore's Indians for the 1950 season, his last as it turned out. He was 12-7 with a 4.65 ERA for the fourth place club that went to the playoff finals. He hit a very respectable .323 with one home run and seventeen RBIs.

BENNIE WARREN

1950, 1951, 1953, 1954 ARDMORE INDIANS, CARDINALS.

Warren was the all-time batting and home run leader in the Sooner State League. His career is discussed at length in Chapter Five.

CARL "JACKIE" SULLIVAN

1952 ARDMORE INDIANS.

Sullivan was signed to manage the 1952 Indians who were starting from scratch upon the remains of the disastrous 1951 McDuff's Seminole Ironmen. Sullivan did not play for the Indians. Sullivan had been bounced around the Texas League and lower classifications until promoted to AAA Buffalo in 1944. Midway through that season, he appeared in one game for the Detroit Tigers. A hard-hitting infielder for the Lubbock Hubbers for the five seasons 1946 through 1950, managing them from 1947 to 1950, he hit .320 for the 1951 Gainesville team in the Big State League. He quit the Indians on May 2, after management refused to pay a $25 fine he earned in a dispute with an umpire in a game at Sherman. At age thirty-four, he signed with Abilene and then begged his release to become manager of Lamesa in the West Texas-New Mexico League. He finished his career in 1955 as a player-manager for Plainview in the same league, hitting .348, .332, and .341 in his final three seasons. He died October 10, 1992.

for the Cardinals. The Cards traded him to the New York Giants in June of 1956. He led the National League in fielding with a .990 average and hit a respectable .298. He won a Golden Glove for his play in left field for the 1959 San Francisco Giants. He was traded to Baltimore for the 1960 season and stayed with the Orioles through 1965. 1966 found him in Philadelphia. He divided his last year between the Phillies and the Astros. Brandt was the original "flake," based on a comment by a teammate that "things seem to flake off his mind and disappear." He retired to his native Omaha.

BOB BLAYLOCK

1953 ARDMORE CARDINALS.

The Chattanooga, Oklahoma, native spent his entire career in the Cardinals organization. He was 1-6 for the 1956 Redbirds after beginning the season at Rochester with a 9-4 record and a 1.67 ERA. After dividing 1957 and 1958 between St. Louis' top two farm teams, Omaha and Rochester, and beginning the 1959 season there, he appeared in three National League games going 0-1 before being sent down to Tulsa in the Texas League. He spent the rest of his career with the Oilers, retiring after the 1962 season.

JACKIE BRANDT

1953 ARDMORE CARDINALS.

Brandt spent six seasons in the Major Leagues winning a Golden Glove in 1959. Jackie Brandt failed to impress the Cardinals' brass with his pitching and after going zero for thirty-six at the plate after becoming an outfielder, he was on the verge of being released. He was assigned to Ardmore and, in his first trip to the plate, hit a line drive home run that finally landed over one hundred feet past the fence. This endeared him to the farm director and launched two careers: his and the player he replaced, Tom Anderson who would become the highest-paid bus driver and trainer in Class D. As a rookie, he hit .257 with twenty-seven home runs and 131 RBIs for the Ardmore team, good enough for a place on the All-Star team. By 1956, he was playing in Busch Stadium

MARTY KUTYNA

1953 ARDMORE CARDINALS.

The third of the 1953 Ardmore Cardinals to reach the Majors, Kutyna was traded after the 1957 season into the Reds' organization with two others for Curt Flood. After 1958 at Seattle of the Pacific Coast League, the Reds traded him to Kansas City where he pitched in four games without decision at the end of the 1959 season following a 14-10 year at AAA Portland. He spent all of 1960 with the A's before being traded for cash and Haywood Sullivan to the expansion Washington Senators where he spent 1961 and 1963. He was 14-16 in 159 American League games in his career with a 3.88 ERA. He finished his baseball career going 2-1 with a 6.00 ERA for the 1963 Buffalo Bisons of the International League.

GENE GREEN

1954 ARDMORE CARDINALS.

In his third season in Organized Ball, Green tore up the Sooner State League in 1954 with thirty-four home runs, 116 RBIs, a .360 batting average, and a place on the All-Star team. He spent five full seasons and parts of two others in the Major Leagues. He was a .267-career hitter in 408 games with the Cardinals, Orioles, Senators, Indians, and Reds. His last season was 1964 divided between the Reds' AAA club at Indianapolis and AA team at Macon, Georgia. He died at age forty-seven in St. Louis on May 23, 1981.

TOM HUGHES

1954 ARDMORE CARDINALS.

Hughes was 8-8 in his rookie year at Ardmore. Following strong seasons at Class C Modesto, where he was 20-6, and Houston of the Texas League posting 18-6 and 14-4 records, Hughes threw in two games for the Cardinals at the end of the 1959 season following a stint in the military. He lost both decisions and posted a 15.75 ERA in four innings. He ended his career at Tulsa in 1961.

GENE OLIVER

1956 ARDMORE CARDINALS.

After beginning his first year in baseball at Albany, Georgia, he tied the Sooner State League record with thirty-nine home runs and was one of four Ardmore Cardinals to be named to the All-Star team. He spent all or part of ten seasons playing 770 games in the National League and sixteen in the American for the Boston Red Sox, hitting a career .246 with ninety-three Big League home runs. He split 1959, 1960, and 1961 between AAA and St. Louis before sticking in the Majors through 1968 with the Braves, Phillies, Red Sox and Cubs. His last year, 1969, began with the Cubs and ended at San Antonio of the Texas League. Oliver was a principal participant in the Randy Hundley Chicago Cubs fantasy baseball camp. He died in Moline, Illinois on March 3, 2007.

JIM MCKNIGHT
1957 ARDMORE CARDINALS.

His .340 average in his second season earned McKnight the League batting title and the slot as the All-Star team's third baseman. In 1958, he jumped from Ardmore to Class AA Houston, and then spent the rest of his career through 1971 playing at the AAA level. He appeared in sixty-three games for the Chicago Cubs in 1960 and 1962, hitting .231 in ninety-one at bats. He was the father of Jeff McKnight who played six seasons for the Mets and Orioles. Jim McKnight died in his native Van Buren County, Arkansas on February 24, 1994.

CHRIS CANNIZZARO
1957 ARDMORE CARDINALS.

He pitched a shutout for Ardmore in his sophomore season. Cannizzaro then spent the rest of his career behind the plate. From 1958 to 1963, he shuttled between AAA and the National League with the Cardinals and Mets, spent 1966, 1967, and part of 1968 in the International League before sticking in the National League through 1974 with Pittsburgh, San Diego, Chicago, and Los Angeles. He had a .236 lifetime batting average and fielded at .983 as a catcher. After a brief 1974 appearance with Hawaii, he sat out the 1975 season, retiring after that. Cannizzaro pitched a few innings without a decision for Salinas of the California League in 1979. He coached the Atlanta Braves from 1976 to 1978. He has the distinction of being an original member of two expansion teams, the New York Mets in 1962 and San Diego Padres in 1969. In 1969, he became the first Padre to be selected as a member of a National League All-Star team.

MICKEY MCGUIRE
1961 ARDMORE ROSEBUDS.

McGuire began the season at Victoria and was called up to Rochester in August. He was a popular player who was twice called up to parent Baltimore: for six games at the end of 1962 and ten games at the close of the 1967 season. He had four hits in seventeen times at bat. He spent the rest of his playing days with Rochester, Seattle and Tucson, all at the AAA level. He hit .277 in thirteen Minor League seasons.

JOHN MILLER

1961 ARDMORE ROSEBUDS.

Miller was a rookie during his year at Ardmore. He recorded twelve Major League wins against fourteen losses in forty-six games over parts of five seasons. The Mets bought his contract from Baltimore in May, 1967 and assigned him to the AAA club at Jacksonville. He ended his career with a 7-7 season in the Carolina League in 1968.

MERLIN NIPPERT

1961 ARDMORE ROSEBUDS.

Oklahoma State University alumnus Merlin Nippert was loaned to the Rosebuds by Boston. He spent ten days with the Red Sox at the end of the 1962 season after a good year at AAA Seattle. He found himself back in Seattle in 1963 and 1964.

JOHN PAPA

1961 ARDMORE ROSEBUDS.

Another bonus baby, John Papa was "good field, no pitch." In two Big League innings with Baltimore, he amassed a 22.50 ERA. He finished his baseball career with Class AA Elmira in 1966.

MARSHALL RENFROE

1961 ARDMORE ROSEBUDS.

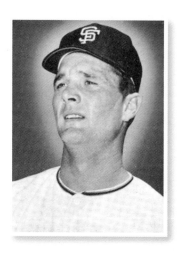

Renfroe had a bitter cup of coffee with the San Francisco Giants on September 27, 1959, giving up six hits including a home run, six earned runs, three walks and three strike outs in two innings. Renfroe was on his way out of Organized Baseball as the benches emptied when he threw at Tulsa's Mike Shannon near the end of the Rosebud's season. He finished his career with Charlotte of the Sally League in 1962. He died on December 10, 1970.

PETE WARD

1961 ARDMORE ROSEBUDS.

Ward led the team in stolen bases with six. He had the most successful career of any Ardmore Rosebud, enjoying nine Major League seasons where he batted .254 with ninety-eight home runs. He followed that with eight seasons as a manager, mainly in the Yankees' organization.

FRANK ZUPO

1961 ARDMORE ROSEBUDS.

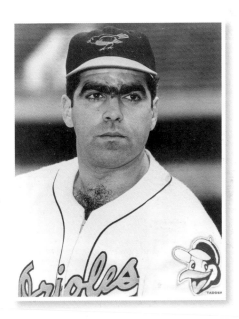

Zupo was a bonus baby who joined Baltimore at age seventeen at the end of the 1957 season. After four years in the Minors, Zupo was called up following the close of the Rosebuds' season, appearing in five games. He ended his baseball career following the 1964 campaign with Dallas in the Pacific Coast League. After baseball he was a fishing guide and owned a wholesale leather goods concern. He died March 25, 2005.

BUSTER NARUM

1961 ARDMORE ROSEBUDS.

Narum had a five-year Major League career mainly as a member of the expansion Washington Senators. He finished baseball with the Tulsa Oilers in 1967. He died May 17, 2004 in Clearwater, Florida.

PERSONALITIES

CHAPTER FIVE

MURL A. "DUTCH" PRATHER

Manager, Ardmore Indians 1947 and Spring Training-July 26, 1949, Pauls Valley Raiders Spring Training-August 2, 1948, Duncan Uttmen July 27-August 22, 1950, McDuff's Seminole Ironmen May 25-Season End 1951.

Murl "Dutch" Prather, an Ada native, managed Ardmore in 1947 and the first part of the 1949 season. He was at the helm for Pauls Valley in its 1948 inaugural season until July 26, when he and the Raiders parted ways. He joined Duncan in 1950 after catcher-manager Hosea Pfeifer was relieved, and continued in that post until Kelly Wingo took over when the team moved to Shawnee. He skippered the 1951 Seminole Ironmen after May 25.

He had a twenty-four-year career in the Minors as a player and manager with twenty-two different teams in fifteen different leagues. Beginning in 1927 with Kingston, Tennessee, of the Virginia League, he reached AA Kansas City in 1931 before being picked up by the Giants' organization. He was invited to the New York Giants 1934 spring camp after a strong year at Nashville. The big first baseman did not stick and was sent back to A-1 Nashville. The Vols traded him to the Dallas Steers of the AA Texas League who in turned traded him to Albany of the AA International

League for 1935. He spent 1936 in Omaha where he was the Western League MVP and 1937 with Sacramento in the Pacific Coast League. He was in semi-pro ball through 1939 after leaving the Solons, playing with Texas Christian University's Heisman winner Sammy Baugh on the 1937 Pampa Oilers finals team. He signed as player-manager of Pampa's 1940 entry in the West Texas-New Mexico League through its move to Amarillo until the league halted play in 1942. During the War years, after receiving a medical discharge following service in the South Pacific, he played in the Southern Association at Atlanta and Little Rock. 1946 found him managing and playing first base for the Tyler Trojans of the East Texas League before heading west to El Paso of the Class B Mexican National League.

He was involved in the formation of the Ardmore baseball club. Prather was business manager, field manager and first baseman during its first year. After leading the Indians to fourth place in the regular season, he took the team to the playoff finals losing to McAlester four games to one. He was hitting at a .436 clip until the early part of August when a one-for-sixteen slump followed by an injury allowed McAlester's Russell Hawley to pass him to claim the batting crown with a .382 average. He finished 1947 at .375.

As Raiders' manager in 1948, after a game at Seminole, he and a local became engaged in a fight that led to Prather receiving a flesh wound from a pistol. He and his assailant were fined for disturbing the peace. At Pauls Valley, his 1948 team languished in the cellar. At the July 21 game, he realized a wish to serve as the public address announcer and let the fans through a local car dealer manage the team. The experiment did not work. He resigned on July 25. He finished the season at first base for Chickasha with a .333 average.

When the Ardmore franchise came up for sale, Dutch Prather got an option to buy the team and planned to incorporate. The Washington Senators would offer a working agreement through Class B Sherman of the Big State League if Prather could arrange to buy the franchise and ballpark. He was unable to put together the deal but was signed as manager for 1949. Hitting .271, he was replaced with the Indians in seventh place.

In the spring of 1950, *The Daily Oklahoman* reported that Prather was looking for any managerial job, pro or semi-pro. On July 27, Otto Utt called on him to guide the hapless Duncan Uttmen while Utt was out with an illness. When the team moved to Shawnee, he handed the reins over to local favorite Kelly Wingo. The next year found him trying to right a floundering independent, McDuff's Seminole Ironmen. His charges ruined his debut with a 4-0 loss at McAlester. Although hitting .414, he was unable to avert the second worst finish in League history, 37-103. On that note he ended both his playing and managerial career.

He returned to farming in Stratford, Oklahoma, but not without tossing his hat in the ring for Sooner State League president at the 1953 annual meeting. He did not receive a nomination. He later turned to umpiring. In addition to 1957 in the Sooner State League, he was umpire-in-chief in the Evangeline League in 1956 where he had called balls and strikes the previous season and later served in the California League. With Ucal Clanton, he established a school for umpires in Ada in March, 1956. He also appeared in the West Texas-New Mexico League in 1953. While his campaign to become League president in 1953 was frustrated, he led the effort to return baseball to Ada after the Herefords' 1955 move to Paris, Texas, and was active in attempts to revive the Sooner State League. He died in Ada at age sixty on March 13, 1967.

BENNIE WARREN

Manager, Ardmore Indians 1950-1951, Sherman Twins 1952, Ardmore Indians and Cardinals 1953-June 15, 1954, Pauls Valley Raiders June 28-Season End 1954.

A native of Elk City, Warren made his home in Oklahoma City. Signed out of high school by John Holland's Oklahoma City Indians, he was farmed out to Lincoln of the Nebraska State League. Warren was business manager and catcher-field manager of the semi-pro Seminole Redbirds at the end of 1936 and in 1937. He returned to the Oklahoma City Indians before being sold to Pittsburgh who in turn sold him to the Phillies in 1938 where he began a Major League career. As a catcher and first baseman, he played through 1947 when he finished at the Polo Grounds with a .219 lifetime average and .980 fielding record as a catcher. He had a detour with the U.S. Navy, playing for the Norman Naval Air Station Skyjackets in 1944 and 1945. He spent 1948 and 1949 in AAA with the Minneapolis Millers and Buffalo Bisons.

Warren began his managerial career in 1950 with the independent Ardmore Indians. He led Ardmore to its best won-lost record ever in 1951 and a regular season championship before losing to McAlester in the playoff finals. When owner Art Willingham moved the franchise to Sherman, he followed and managed the 1952 Twins to a fifth-place finish. Waco Turner prevailed on Willingham to release Warren to manage the Ardmore club that was coming off a disastrous 1952 season. He took the 1953 Indians with Jackie Brandt and Al Viotta to a first-place finish but could not get past the McAlester jinx in the playoffs. He was ejected from more games in 1953 than any other player or manger in the League. He managed the 1954 Cardinals to seventh place when he was replaced on June 16 by Frank Mancuso as part of a general reorganization. He relieved Lloyd Pearson at Pauls Valley on June 28, 1954, but was unable to pull them out of the cellar. The final edition of the Raiders finished in eighth place.

He held the League's all-time record for career batting average and home runs, edging Pauls Valley's Donnie Williamson in both categories. He was named the manager of the 1951 All-Star team and the catcher on the 1952 and 1953 teams. He was a policeman in Seminole before World War II. After the Pauls Valley stint, he returned to Oklahoma City where he was a jailer for the Oklahoma County sheriff. He died in Oklahoma City on May 11, 1994.

HUGH WILLINGHAM

Manager, Seminole Oilers July 2, 1947-July 26, 1949, Ardmore Indians May 5-July 8, 1952.

The only Major Leaguer born in Dalhart, Texas, he was an all-state football, basketball and baseball player at El Reno, Oklahoma. He hit .238 in his 1930 rookie season with the White Sox followed by 1931-1933 with the Phillies. Philadelphia sold him to the AA

Kansas City Blues on May 5, 1933, who dealt him to the Oklahoma City Indians. He enjoyed two good seasons in 1934 and 1935 as a regular third baseman at Sioux City in the Western League. He spent the rest of the 1930s playing semi-pro ball for the Enid Eason Oilers and Duncan-based Halliburton Oil Cementers, returning to Organized Ball in 1941 after the Cementers were discontinued. His first year back was a good one when he hit .349 at Borger in the West Texas-New Mexico League. The next season he was manager and second baseman for the Gassers where he was hitting .452 when the league folded in 1942. He then signed with the seventh-place Oklahoma City Indians for the rest of the last season before the Texas League suspended operations. He spent 1944 and 1945 in the Pacific Coast League with the Los Angeles Angels and Hollywood Stars. 1946 found him managing the Ft. Smith Giants to the Western Association pennant. Signed to manage and play for Odessa in 1947, he asked to be released from his contract because he could not find housing for his family there; he was hitting .361 after forty-seven games. He last played the infield in Odessa.

After advertising in *The Sporting News*, Cy Fenolio signed him to manage his Seminole Oilers. He served until the last third of the 1949 season when relieved by Paul Schoendienst, then a scout for the White Sox. In addition to pinch hitting, he pitched in relief all of the seasons he managed in the Sooner State League.

He was the master of the "Blooper Ball" and, with good control, was 19-13 with a 2.42 ERA. He talked to batters while on the mound causing more than a few to lose their concentration. As an umpire, he was best known for his quip during a game between the University of Oklahoma and Oklahoma A&M in 1951. After having hit two home runs in the game, Cowboy slugger Joe Buck came to the plate a third time. Willingham called two close pitches balls with Buck drawing a walk. The Sooner catcher complained "You sure put him on base that time" to which he replied "They were close but you gotta' give me credit—I held him to one base."

A favorite in Seminole, he joined the Sheriff's Department of Seminole County, Oklahoma, after leaving the Sooner State League. When Fred McDuff gave up after the 1951 season, Willingham actively worked to get the team moved to Duncan rather than Ardmore. He organized a sandlot team sponsored by Petroleum Machine of Seminole after that. In June of 1952, Willingham resigned his position as deputy sheriff to become the third of five mangers of the 1952 Ardmore Indians. He quit on July 8, 1952, with the Indians in last place. He was superintendent of Oilers Park in 1954, and business manager of the Oilers in 1955. By 1959, he was an agent with the Oklahoma crime bureau and later Undersheriff of Canadian County He died on June 15, 1988, at age eighty-two, and is interred in El Reno, Oklahoma.

FRANK MANCUSO

Manager, Ardmore Cardinals June 16, 1954-1955.

A member of the 1944 American League champion St. Louis Browns, he hit for a career average of .241 as a catcher with the Browns and Washington Senators. Before then, his eighteen-year career began in 1937 in the Browns' farm system through which he advanced from the Western

Association St. Joseph team to the 1942 San Antonio Missions of the AA Texas League. He spent 1948 through1951 in Class AAA with Toledo and Baltimore and AA at San Antonio and Beaumont. He managed Wichita Falls' Class B Big State League entry in 1952 and took over his hometown Houston Buffalos of the Texas League in 1953, making his connection with the Cardinals' system. He came out of retirement to take over the Ardmore Cardinals from Bennie Warren on June 16, 1954, and stayed through the next season. His career high batting average was .333 with the 1954 Ardmore Cardinals. At the close of the 1955 season, his rhubarb with plate umpire Lee Hanning resulted in a 9-0 forfeiture of the fifth-place Cardinals to Seminole.

He left baseball after his tenure at Ardmore and moved into the more dangerous world of politics. He served thirty years on the Houston City Council. Harris County built the Frank Mancuso Sports Complex, a facility that strategically reaches out to the needs of inner-city children, in his honor. He was inducted into the Texas Baseball Hall of Fame in 2003. He retired and lived near his home town of Houston, Texas. He died at age eighty-nine in Pasadena, Texas on August 4, 2007.

J. C. DUNN

Manager, Ardmore Cardinals 1956 and 1957; Ardmore Rosebuds 1961.

Dunn, referred to by friends as Howard, was a star athlete at Spiro, Oklahoma, and then became a boxer in the Navy. He played football and baseball at Southeastern State in Durant as well as semi-pro ball with the Durant G.I.s. The Washington Senators signed him in 1948 after a tryout with Sherman-Denison and sent him to Lebanon, Tennessee, where he was hitting .400 before hurting his knee, and

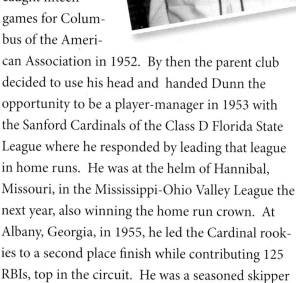

earning his release. The Cardinals picked him up. He was headed for Houston of the Texas League in 1950 when he broke an arm and aggravated his bad knee. He caught fifteen games for Columbus of the American Association in 1952. By then the parent club decided to use his head and handed Dunn the opportunity to be a player-manager in 1953 with the Sanford Cardinals of the Class D Florida State League where he responded by leading that league in home runs. He was at the helm of Hannibal, Missouri, in the Mississippi-Ohio Valley League the next year, also winning the home run crown. At Albany, Georgia, in 1955, he led the Cardinal rookies to a second place finish while contributing 125 RBIs, top in the circuit. He was a seasoned skipper when he took over the Class D Ardmore team.

In 1956, his first season, he took the Cardinals to a regular season pennant and playoff finals and, again, led the League in RBIs with 134. In 1957 at age thirty-one and the oldest player in the League, he guided the team to the last playoff championship after a second place finish during the regular season. He is most remembered for having suffered two gunshot wounds at the hands of a Ponca City bellman who claimed some of the Cardinals had made a racial slur at the hotel and roughed him up.

The Associated Press reported the incident under the headline "Gunfire in Ponca City." Before some 400 fans on August 8, Dunn had just scored a run in the second inning. Five shots that could be heard over the radio broadcast of the game were fired striking Dunn in the side and leg. The target was outfielder Coy Smith, who was released after the incident never to play again. "As soon as the shooting began, Smith headed in full flight for center field." The assault on the porter, James Johnson, as related by Hall of Famer Billy Williams is far different than the "good-natured roughhousing" described by the Ardmore players. Dunn recovered in time to relieve Mike Ryba on August 22, and hit an amazing .593 in the post-season as the Cardinals swept through the last Sooner State League playoff, first eliminating the Muskogee Giants and then the first place Paris Orioles.

Dunn continued as a player-manager with Dothan and Pensacola of the Alabama-Florida League from 1958 through 1960. In late August, 1961, he signed as a free agent at the end of the season with the injury-plagued Texas League Ardmore Rosebuds. He hit .188 in a four game local comeback.

He settled in Ardmore after his playing days. For the next eleven years he was a shop teacher and baseball coach of the Ardmore High School Tigers. On October 24, 1973, on the heels of an all-night card playing session and after leaving school following first hour, Dunn was murdered by a shot gun blast as he struggled with his assailant in the bathroom of his home. The suspected motive was theft of a large amount of cash. He was forty-seven. The murder has never been solved.

MIKE RYBA

Manager, Ardmore Cardinals
August 10-21, 1957.

The Cardinal and Red Sox veteran hurler (and catcher) who began pro ball in 1925 was called in on an emergency basis to handle the Cardinals after manager J. C. Dunn was shot on August 8, 1957. The Cardinals went into a slump, giving up a wide lead to finish one-half game behind the Paris Orioles. With Dunn back at the helm, the Cardinals swept the Orioles in the playoffs to capture the last Sooner State League championship. Ryba was recalled by historian Harry Berry: "Mike Ryba was the epitome of the journeyman ballplayer. Once in the minors –name any league, Mike was in it—he demonstrated his versatility by playing a different position each inning and, when the game was over, by driving the team bus to the train." He died on December 13, 1971, from a fall while trimming trees at his home in Springfield, Missouri.

ARTHUR WILLINGHAM

Owner, Ardmore Indians 1950-1951,
Sherman and Sherman-Denison
Twins 1952-1953, Tri-City Oilers
January 1-June 24, 1954

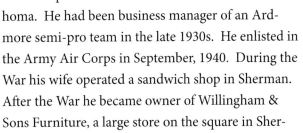

Art Willingham was born into a railroad family in Haskell County, Oklahoma, and raised in the oil patch in southern Oklahoma. He had been business manager of an Ardmore semi-pro team in the late 1930s. He enlisted in the Army Air Corps in September, 1940. During the War his wife operated a sandwich shop in Sherman. After the War he became owner of Willingham & Sons Furniture, a large store on the square in Sherman. He also owned a drilling rig and operated a contract drilling business. In 1948, he drilled a successful rank wildcat well on the north side of Sherman that allowed him to indulge his baseball interests. Sometime between 1959 and 1961, the Willinghams left Sherman for Oklahoma City.

He got into the professional baseball business in 1946 when he was awarded one of the franchises in the new Class C East Texas League. That season he gave Monty Stratton, the White Sox pitcher whose career came to a tragic end in a 1938 hunting accident, a comeback chance where he was 18-8, a remarkable feat for a one-legged man. When the Class B Big State League, a group of north and central Texas cities that operated through 1957, was organized in 1947 he moved his club up a Class. Adopting the cities of Sherman and Denison, Willingham called his teams the "Twins." He had built a new ball park for the 1946 season. The venue named Twins Park favored hitters with fences 320 feet down the lines and 375 feet to center. He sold the Twins at a profit to a group of local investors in the early part of the 1947 season. He retained a minority interest and served as an advisor.

A player dispute brought Art Willingham to the attention of the President of the National Association. Pitcher J. R. Mosley, who had gone 0-2 for the 1942 Ft. Worth Cats, filed a claim through the National Association for $600 of an $800 signing bonus. He produced a contract dated February 12, 1947, signed by Willingham. The player received a bonus of $200 on signing and was to receive $200 on April 15, May 15, and June 15. Willingham refused to pay saying "Before we got the deal made, I found out his arm was bad" and claimed that contract had yet to be to be mailed

and had been torn up. Alternatively, Willingham claimed if Mosley had a contract for a bonus, he was not supposed to. President George Trautman ruled that because bonuses had to be registered with the National Association, and this was not, the Sherman-Denison team had to pay Mosley $600. But since Willingham had sold the franchise and the new owners were innocent he denied Mosley's request for free agency status. Because Willingham was out of Organized Baseball, the National Association had no jurisdiction to fine him. Mosley, incidentally, never pitched again. Despite that, in 1954 Trautman said of Willingham "he is one of the most diligent and conscientious club owners in the lower minors. One that you can be sure that if he makes a commitment it will be kept to the letter."

When the owners of the Ardmore Indians were preparing to forfeit the franchise, Willingham was allowed to purchase the team following the 1949 season. The price was his agreement to assume the roughly $5,000 of accumulated debt of the club. He named his son, Bobby, general manager and opened shop at 30 ½ N. Washington in Ardmore. Journeyman Glenn Snyder soon took over. His Ardmore teams were independents and relied heavily on the "Cambria pipeline" of Latin American, especially Cuban, players. He hired former Major League catcher Bennie Warren to manage. Under his leadership the Indians finished fourth in 1950 before 44,454 fans, losing to McAlester in the playoff final. The 1951 team won the pennant with a .712 win percentage before dropping the playoff final again to McAlester. Attendance, however, slipped to 40,742.

He put the franchise up for sale after Ardmore voters turned down a bond issue to build a new baseball facility. When no buyer emerged, he sought and was granted permission to move the team to his hometown of Sherman. By this time, Twins Park was six years old. Run down, it needed between $10,000 and $15,000 in repairs and improvements. Arturo Gonzalez —who became the ball park's owner in 1951 when he bought the Big State League franchise— agreed to lease it to its builder, Willingham, for $1 with Willingham paying insurance and Gonzalez the taxes.

Continuing to operate as an independent, the 1952 Sherman Twins and 1953 Sherman-Denison Twins finished fifth and sixth. Worse still, attendance slumped from 60,000 in 1951, to 18,000 and 19,000 in the next two years. Player sales in both years brought the bottom line to near break even. After the 1953 season, Willingham was no longer willing to feed the beast but was unable to walk away. At the February, 1954, League meeting, he was allowed to move the Twins to Seminole, Oklahoma.

Seminole had been out of the League since the Ironmen moved to Ardmore following the 1951 season. He decided to name his club "Tri-City" because he planned to play the last half of the season in Holdenville and Wewoka. This did not come to fruition, however. With the franchise tottering on the verge of bankruptcy and the players all becoming free agents if they were not paid by June 27, Willingham sold the club to local Seminole interests.

He just could not put Oklahoma behind him, though. Former Sooner State League President, Ucal Clanton, sued him on July 11, 1957, for failure to convey a 1/16 interest in an oil well. After a trial, Clanton won. He enjoyed some success including re-opening a dry well in Creek County to discover a commercial field. He had been a gambler in the oil patch and in the baseball business. He was also a professional gambler. Before 1968, Willingham

operated a gambling operation including craps and blackjack in Canadian County, Oklahoma. He was arrested in 1969 and again, in a large bust, in July, 1970, along with son, Bobby and several others. He apparently later broke the gaming habit. When he died on April 1, 1991, in Bethany, Oklahoma at age eighty-six, his occupation was listed as restaurant owner.

In retrospect, Willingham's greatest contribution to the League was breaking the color barrier. Napoleon Daniels took the mound for Sherman on June 25, 1952, and hurled the Twins to a 7-6 victory over Chickasha. He soon signed another black pitcher, Carl "Strawberry" Newberry. Other teams in the League quickly followed. Jim Crow was still a fact de jure in both Texas and Oklahoma, and black players in the League were treated as second class team members as were the fans in the "Negro Bleachers". It still was a courageous gesture to be the first owner in six seasons to break with segregation.

WACO TURNER

Club President, Ardmore Cardinals 1953-1955.

Born in Mississippi on February 15, 1891, his parents moved to the Chickasaw Nation before 1900 where they settled as farmers. The 1910 Census shows him as a hired hand of the Taylor family in Burneyville, Oklahoma. Turner learned to be a school teacher at Southeastern State College in Durant, Oklahoma, where Lloyd Noble, Ardmore oil man and philanthropist, was also earning a diploma. Following his return from World War I, he was teaching in the little Love County school at Overbrook when in 1918 he met and married the love of his life, Texas school teacher, O.P. (Opie) James. Riding home on a horse one day in 1921, he caught the smell of oil and spent all he had leasing up minerals in Love and Carter counties. The oil gamble paid off handsomely. He and Opie became members of Ardmore's new oil wealthy. Then he discovered cotton, and lost his oil fortune on that gamble.

The year 1931 found Waco and Opie living in a tent in Gregg County, Texas, purchasing mineral leases behind the discoveries of C. M. "Dad" Joiner, who discovered the East Texas field when the Daisy Bradford No. 3 came in on October 5, 1930. Turner's properties and leases became the basis for his second fortune. In the 1940s and 1950s, the Turners were earning $80,000 per day, banking it in Dallas, and trying to spend it as fast as it came in. Opie and Waco lived a relatively modest life in a city of oil millionaires, Ardmore, Oklahoma. Their extravagances were the high life in Florida, gifts to friends and associates, his beloved Dornick Hills Country Club in Ardmore, his compound and golf course at Burneyville, Oklahoma, the PGA and LPGA tournaments they underwrote, and baseball.

Turner was one of the original Sooner State League organizers at the September, 1946, meeting. He turned over the franchise to the Ardmore Athletic Association before the League was firmly organized. He was not involved when Ardmore Baseball Club, Inc., a community-based group of investors led by restaurateur Lou Priddy and banker John Judd, purchased the team.

Responding to Art Willingham's relocation of the Ardmore club to Sherman, jeweler W.C. Peden and A. P. "Pink" Shuman organized Ardmore Baseball Association as a non-profit corporation in February, 1952, to acquire the Seminole franchise. As the independent non-profit floundered in its first season, Waco Turner was elected president in November, 1952, to turn around things. He reasoned that golf is an expensive game that most people cannot afford but nearly everyone could afford a couple of nights at the ball park each week.

He first negotiated a working agreement with the St. Louis Cardinals, beating out Shawnee and Miami of the K-O-M League that had been chasing after the last place in the Cardinals' farm system. Turner flew to St. Louis, walked into the Cards' office unannounced and was immediately ushered into the office of vice president William Walsingham, Jr. With owner Fred Saigh under indictment for tax evasion, he was running the club while Saigh was negotiating a plea agreement. Walsingham thought Turner was there to buy the Cardinals. Turner explained he just wanted to put a winning team in Ardmore and that a working agreement with St. Louis could do that. Within an hour, the Ardmore Indians became the Cardinals. Waco became actively involved in affairs of the Sooner State League. Always domineering, when the League did not concur with his insistence that a team be placed in Duncan rather than Paris, Texas, he turned the franchise back to A.P. Shuman and the Ardmore Baseball Association after the 1955 season. His perceived betrayal by the Dornick Hills directors and membership coupled with his involvement in building his Burneyville resort were contributing causes for walking away from baseball.

A. P. SHUMAN

Club President, Ardmore Cardinals 1955-1957,
Ardmore Rosebuds 1961.

Anson Pink Shuman was an Ardmore native whose name and face were synonymous with baseball in the city. Returning from World War II, he re-joined the family business, Shuman-Dayton Machine Co. As a member of the executive committee of the Ardmore American Legion Post, he was the director for American Legion baseball. Along with W. C. Peden, he secured the transfer of the Seminole franchise after Art Willingham moved the original Indians to Sherman. He served on the board of the Ardmore Baseball Association from then until shortly before his death on September 20, 1961. When Waco Turner resigned as president in 1955, Shuman assumed that position. He was responsible for the building of Cardinal Park. As president of the Association, he was intimately involved with the attempts to revive the League after the 1957 season. He promoted a regular season Texas League game between Houston and Tulsa in 1958 that drew an overflow 3,100 ticket holders to 2,800-capacity Cardinal Park. Having shown that the town could draw fans for good baseball, Derrest Williams had no difficulty in persuading the other Texas League owners to move his Victoria Rosebuds franchise to Ardmore on May 26, 1961. Led by Shuman, Ardmore Baseball Association assumed local operation of the Rosebuds for the summer. Failing health forced his withdrawal as president. On August 10, before the game with Tulsa, 1,384 friends and fans packed Cardinal Park for A. P. Shuman night where he was recognized for his years of service to the community.

GARY DON BIGHAM

Batboy, Ardmore 1952, 1953.

Only child Gary Bigham was one of three batboys —Derril McGuire and Red Warren, the manager's son, were the others— who began the 1953 season with the Ardmore team. Bigham and McGuire earned their positions by selling season tickets, Bigham at his parents' laundry and McGuire from his father's barber shop. Waco Turner paid the Indians' batboys $2.50 per game when Ardmore won. Bigham was a batboy from 1952 until his death the following year. An honor student, Boy Scout, and promising baseball player, he accidentally hanged himself at home on July 11, 1953, eight days short of his fourteenth birthday. His baseball teammates served as pall bearers.

HAROLD "RED" SOLLARS

Ardmore 1947-1949

In many ways, Red Sollars was a paradigm for the young men who came through the Sooner State League after World War II. He played two years in a Major League organization before being released —in his case because of an injury suffered while playing for Iola, Kansas. He married a local girl from Ardmore and went to work in his father-in-law's plumbing business during the off-season. Following his release, he pursued the dream a bit longer with three different independent clubs at or close to his new home. With a growing family, he hung up his spikes. Escaping from the plumbing business, he went on to earn a college degree and teaching certificate to match his wife's. He raised five daughters, all of whom became teachers.

Born in St. Joseph, Missouri, Sollars signed with the Cleveland organization and was assigned to the Indians' new Class D affiliate in Ardmore. He played shortstop and third base in his short professional career. He was a hustler, always slid on his stomach, and reputedly no one finished a game as sweaty or dirty. He played all of 1947 there. He had a sixteen-game hitting streak that was the League standard in that first season. He began the 1948 season with the Cleveland affiliate at Class C Burlington, Iowa, of the Central Association, but after a .195 start was sent down to Iola, Kansas, of the Class D K-O-M

League on May 25. He was there long enough to bat in eight runs and get hurt. He was released and returned to his wife's home town of Ardmore where he finished the season with the Indians. He divided his last season among three teams. Beginning with Class B Gainesville, Texas, of the Big State League, he was soon sent down to Clovis, N.M. of the Class C West Texas-New Mexico League where he hit .269 with fifteen RBIs. A free agent again, he returned to Ardmore to finish his third season there batting .214 with eleven RBIs and one home run. He played semi-pro ball for the Ardmore Blue Jays. As owner of Sollars Sporting Goods on South Washington Street, he arranged for an Ardmore pick up team to play Satchel Paige's Caribbean Kings at Cardinal Park on May 27, 1960. He later set up a fast pitch softball league. Sollars taught and coached at Ardmore High School where former Ardmore player-manager Howard "J. C." Dunn was also on the faculty. He and his family moved to Havasu City, Arizona, in 1967. He died there in September, 1999.

ERNESTO KLEIN

Ardmore 1949-1952

Ernie Klein is an exemplar of the dozens of players from Cuba that passed through the Sooner State League. He spent his entire playing career in Class D with independent teams. He hit well enough and was improving his ball handling when an injury broke his dream of making it to "the Show." He went back to Cuba for a life outside baseball. Like a number of Cubans, he fled Castro's revolutionary regime for the United States, became a citizen, and has enjoyed the American dream.

Born to Hungarian Jewish immigrants in Havana, Cuba, at age eighteen Ernesto Wallerstein Klein was signed mid-summer in 1948 by Joe

64

Cambria to a Washington minor league contract and optioned to Big Spring, Texas, in the Longhorn League where he hit a respectable .255, fielded .922 at second base and .838 at third. For all or part of the next three seasons, Klein was to become the post-war record holder for games played on an Ardmore team with 401. In 1949, he appeared in fifty-six games at second base for Dutch Prather until he broke his left hand, going on the disabled list for the remainder of the season. Back with Ardmore in 1950, Bennie Warren moved him to the hot corner for the third-place Indians. He enjoyed his best season in 1951 with the best team in Ardmore's and the League's history playing mainly in the outfield and dividing third base duties with Hector Bonet and Darrell Pierce.

As a veteran in 1952, he began the season at Vernon in the Longhorn League where he found his glove at third base but was soon back in Ardmore in the outfield laboring for the worst team in Ardmore's history and a contender for one of the weakest in League history. He left spring training in 1953 with the Morristown, Tennessee, Red Sox, a club

loaded with Cubans including thrower Pete Ramos who would come up to the Washington Senators in 1955 to begin a fifteen-year Big League career. Only seven games into the season, he suffered a career-ending injury to his right arm.

Returning to Havana, he married and began a business installing air conditioners in automobiles. A year after the overthrow of the Batista government, the Klein family joined the exodus to the United States. Settling in New York, and using his middle name Wallerstein, he spent thirty-seven years in the graphics department for the late investment giant Merrill Lynch. Following retirement, they settled in Lakewood, New Jersey.

ARMIN SOMONTE

Ardmore 1949-1951

The string bean Turk from Caimguey, Cuba, at 135 pounds Somonte was the best pitcher to appear for Ardmore with a 3.23 ERA for a 53-35 record over three seasons and the only Sooner State League pitcher to log two no-hitters. He was the first Indian to win twenty games —twenty-four in

1951— and holds the Ardmore record for most wins in a season. He twirled his first no-hitter in the seven-inning nightcap of the June 13, 1949 game with League-leading Pauls Valley, allowing only three base runners on two walks and an error for a 6-0 decision. He tossed his second no-hit, no run game against Lawton on August 8, 1951, an 18-0 gem. The southpaw set the League record for strikeouts, 341, that year as well. Willingham sold him to Tyler for $2,500 in the fall. He

helped the Tyler East Texans on the way to the Big
State League playoff before being sent, along with
Ardmore team mate Joe Nodar, to Texas City in the
Class B Gulf Coast League going 7-9 for a last place
independent. He finished his playing days in 1953
with the Port Arthur Seahawks recording a 13-14
tally for a losing club. He returned to Cuba after his
American baseball career.

TOM ANDERSON

1953-1958

A slow-talking Marietta, Oklahoma, native
who had played semi-pro ball, Tom Anderson
declined to sign a contract with a professional team
because of the job insecurity. He had earned and
lost a job earlier when he became the youngest
member of the Oklahoma House of Representatives
in 1948, and was defeated for re-election in 1950.

Waco Turner, new president of the Ardmore ball club, wanted the twenty-six-year old Anderson and offered him job security if he would sign on with the Indians. The deal made was that if Anderson did not make the team after spring training, Turner would hire him. Giving up a steady job, Anderson —the first player the new-look Ardmore club signed— traveled to Albany, Georgia, home of the Cardinals' Minor League camp. He played well enough to make the squad until Jackie Brandt appeared. Released the day before the regular season, Waco Turner, true to his word, hired him to serve as team trainer and bus driver.

Anderson worked for Turner during the off-season. After he trained with the Fresno Cardinals during the spring of 1954, he drove the bus back to Ardmore with manager Bennie Warren's charges. He remained in the job through the 1957 season serving with managers Frank Mancuso and J.C. Dunn. Following C. P. Sebastian's resignation as business manager, in January, 1958, the Ardmore Cardinals' directors tapped Anderson to become, as it turned out, the last business manager. When the ball club folded, Anderson continued in Waco Turner's employ building the Burneyville golf resort.

Later moving with his family to Oklahoma City, he died there in 1983. Before his death, he gave his collection of photographs to his roommate on road trips, senior bat boy and by then practicing attorney, Derril McGuire of Ardmore.

PHOTO CREDITS

References are to page number. The Author owns a number of snapshots and publicity photos that appear in the book. Photos appearing in the Author's book *Baseball in the Cross Timbers: The Story of the Sooner State League* are indicated in bold type and appear courtesy of the Author and the Oklahoma Heritage Association. There are several contributors other than the Author who provided multiple photos. These are *The Daily Ardmoreite* ("Ardmoreite"), *Derril McGuire* ("McGuire"), *Mrs. Betty Anderson* ("Anderson"), *Ernesto Wallerstein* ("Klein") and *Barbara Sessions* ("Sessions"). Every effort has been made to utilize only photos that are in the public domain or for which permissions has previously been received.

8. (upper) Steven Harris; (lower) Sessions

9. Becca Smith Hagli

10. (inset) **Brent Horton's Tyler, Texas, Minor League History;** (lower) **Sylvia Moore**

11. Author's Collection

12. (left) Ardmoreite; (right) **John G. Hall**

13. (inset) **John G. Hall; (below) McGuire**

14. (upper left) Roger Willingham; (lower left) **Stephens County Historical Museum;** (right) Bobby Cramer

15. **Laurie Anne Williams**

16. (left) **Klein;** (right) **Historical**

Museum of Pottawatomie County and Santa Fe Historical Museum

18. (left) **Klein;** (right) Ardmoreite

19. **Klein**

20. **Klein**

21. (both) *Seminole Producer*

22. © Brace Photos by permission.

23. (upper) Courtesy National Baseball Hall of Fame Library, Cooperstown, N.Y.; (lower) **John G. Hall**

25. (upper left and right) Ardmoreite; (lower left) Sylvia Moore

26. (upper) Sylvia Moore; (middle) **McGuire;** (lower left) Anderson

26-27 (lower) **McGuire**

27. **McGuire and Sessions**

28. (upper) **Anderson;** (lower) **McGuire**

29. (all) **McGuire**

30. (upper) Sessions; (lower left) **McGuire;** (lower right) Ardmoreite

31. **McGuire** identification by Sessions

32. Sessions

33. Sessions

34. Author © 2008

35. (upper inset) www.mcalesterphotos.com; (lower) **McGuire**

36. **Anson Shuman and Ardmoreite**

37. *The Paris News*

38. Author's Collection

39. **Anson Shuman and Ardmoreite**

40. (both) Ardmoreite

41. (upper) **Oklahoma Heritage Association and** *The Daily Oklahoman*; (inset) www.picasaweb.google.com/WrightWingOOTP/1943; (lower right) Ardmoreite

42. (upper right) Ardmoreite; (lower left) **Ardmoreite;** (lower right) *Pauls Valley Daily Democrat*

43. (all) Ardmoreite

44. (left) **Texas League of Professional Baseball Clubs;** (right) Ardmoreite

45. Ardmoreite

46. (upper) Ardmoreite; (lower) Aaron Tallent and Mrs. Doyle May

48. (upper left) © Brace Photos by permission; (lower left) **Royse Parr;** (upper right) Courtesy National Baseball Hall of Fame and Museum; (lower right) Courtesy 2000 Cups of Coffee (SABR 2009)

49. (left) **Author's Collection;** (right) **McGuire**

50. (upper left) © Brace Photos by permission; (lower left) Courtesy National Baseball Hall of Fame Library, Cooperstown, N.Y;. (upper right) **McGuire;** (lower right) Courtesy National Baseball Hall of Fame Library, Cooperstown, N.Y.

51. (upper) **McGuire;** (middle) Author's Collection; (lower) Courtesy National Baseball Hall of Fame Library, Cooperstown, N.Y.

52. (upper left) Courtesy National Baseball Hall of Fame Library, Cooperstown, N.Y.; (lower left) © Brace Photos by permission; (upper right) © Brace Photos by permission; (lower right) **Author's Collection**

53. (upper) Author's Collection; (middle and lower) Courtesy National Baseball Hall of Fame Library, Cooperstown, N.Y.

54. Spalding Official Baseball Guide 1931

56. (left) **McGuire;** (right) © Brace Photos by permission

57. **McGuire**

58. **McGuire**

59. (upper) Courtesy National Baseball Hall of Fame Library, Cooperstown, N.Y.; (lower) **Klein**

61. **McGalliard Collection, Ardmore Public Library**

63. (upper) Sessions; (lower) **Laurie Anne Williams**

64. **Harold Sollars family**

65. (both) **Klein**

66. (both) **Anderson**

BIBLIOGRAPHY

Adelson, Bruce, *Brushing Back Jim Crow*, Charlottesville: Univ. of Va. Press, 1999

Bridges, Butch, *This 'N That*, comp. at http://www.oklahomahistory.net/

Burke, Bob, Kenny Frank, and Royse Parr, *Glory Days of Summer: The History of Baseball in Oklahoma*, Oklahoma City: Oklahoma Heritage Association, 1999

Gray Sally M., *Territory Town: The Ardmore Story*, Ardmore, OK: privately published, 2006

Heritage Microfilm, *Newspaper Archives*, http://www.newspaperarchives.com

Johnson, Lloyd and Miles Wolff ed., *The Encyclopedia of Minor League Baseball* 2d ed. Durham, NC: Baseball America, Inc., 1997

Old-Time Data, Inc., version 6.0, *Professional Baseball Player Data Base*

Paper of Record.Com, *Paper of Record*, http://www.paperofrecord.com

Pierce, Peter G., *Baseball in the Cross Timbers: The Story of the Sooner State League*, Oklahoma City: Oklahoma Heritage Association, 2009

Selko, Jamie, *Minor League All Star Teams, 1922-1962*, Jefferson, N.C.: McFarland, 2007

Society for American Baseball Research, *SABR Minor Leagues Database*, http://www.baseball-reference.com/minors

Spalding's Official Baseball Guide 1931

Sports Reference LLC, *Baseball-Reference*, http://www.baseball-reference.com/

Spink, J. G. Taylor, *Official Baseball Guide*, St. Louis: Charles C. Spink & Son, 1947-1962

Sullivan, Neil *The Minors*, New York: St. Martin's, 1990

The Daily Ardmoreite 1946-1961, microfilm collection, Chickasaw Regional Library, Ardmore branch

INDEX

Bold type indicates photograph or illustration of subject.